What's So Funny?

Choreography and Dance Studies

A series of books edited by Muriel Topaz and Robert P. Cohan, C.B.E.

Volume 1
The Life and Times of Ellen von Frankenberg
Karen Bell-Kanner

Volume 2
Dooplé
The Eternal Law of African Dance
Alphonse Tiérou

Volume 3
Elements of Performance
A Guide for Performers in Dance, Theatre and Opera
Pauline Koner

Volume 4
Upward Panic
The Autobiography of Eva Palmer-Sikelianos
Edited by John P. Anton

Volume 5
Modern Dance in Germany and the United States
Crosscurrents and Influences
Isa Partsch-Bergsohn

Volume 6
Antonio de Triana and the Spanish Dance
A Personal Recollection
Rita Vega de Triana

Volume 7
The Dance of Death
Kurt Jooss and the Weimar Years
Suzanne K. Walther

Volume 8
Dance Words
Compiled by Valerie Preston-Dunlop

Volume 9
East Meets West in Dance: Voices in the Cross-Cultural Dialogue
Edited by Ruth Solomon and John Solomon

Please see the back of this book for other titles in the Choreography and Dance Studies series

What's So Funny?

Sketches from My Life

Lotte Goslar

harwood academic publishers
Australia • Canada • China • France • Germany • India
Japan • Luxembourg • Malaysia • The Netherlands • Russia
Singapore • Switzerland • Thailand

Copyright © 1998 OPA (Overseas Publishers Association) Amsterdam B.V. Published under license under the Harwood Academic Publishers imprint, part of The Gordon and Breach Publishing Group.

All rights reserved.

No part of this book may be reproduced or utilized in any form or by any means, electronic or mechanical, including photocopying and recording, or by any information storage or retrieval system, without permission in writing from the publisher.

Amsteldijk 166
1st Floor
1079 LH Amsterdam
The Netherlands

British Library Cataloguing in Publication Data

Goslar, Lotte
  What's so funny?: sketches from my life. – (Choreography and dance studies; v. 15)
  1. Goslar, Lotte 2. Mimes – Germany – Biography
  I. Title
  792.3'092

ISBN 90-5702-177-3

Cover illustration by Lotte Goslar

Contents

Clowns. Six Sketches by Lotte Goslar	v–xiv
Introduction to the Series	ix
Illustrations	xi
Lotte Goslar – For Instance, a Clown, by Horst Koegler	xv
Emigration	xvii
An Explanation	xxi
How Sweet It Is	1
First Memories	5
Palucca	13
So Much Luck (I)	17
The Disgruntled	21
Up and Out	25
The Peppermill Theater	29
The Liberated Theater	33
The Dancing Clown, by Voskovec and Werich	39
The Fortune Teller	41
Off to America	43
A Propos Aging	48
So Much Luck (II)	51
On Tour: Road Signs	57
To The Rescue	65
A New World	71
The Turnabout Theater	75
My Film Career	81
Cats I've Met	87
The Dancing Hausfrau	95
Lotte Goslar's *Circus Scene*, by Joel Schechter	97
TV	107
Magic	109
Not So Magic	111
A New Experience	115
Marilyn	117
A Large Landscape	121

What's So Funny?	123
Solos	125
The Company	137
Letters	145
List of Works	157
Portraits	163
Index	165

Introduction to the Series

Choreography and Dance Studies is a book series of special interest to dancers, dance teachers and choreographers. Focusing on dance composition, its techniques and training, the series will also cover the relationship of choreography to other components of dance performance such as music, lighting and the training of dancers.

In addition, *Choreography and Dance Studies* will seek to publish new works and provide translations of works not previously published in English, as well as to publish reprints of currently unavailable books of outstanding value to the dance community.

Muriel Topaz
Robert P. Cohan

Illustrations

Right heel, right toe, etc.	5
My mother	7
The toddler	9
Lotte Goslar as *Femme Fatale*	19
Lotte Goslar as *The Disgruntled*	20
Lotte Goslar in 1938	22
Lotte Goslar back in Europe	23
Lotte Goslar as *The Wood Sprite*	26
Lotte Goslar as *The Wood Sprite*	26
Lotte Goslar as *The Artist in Person*	27
Werich and Voskovec	34
Balada z Hadrů: a program from The Liberated Theater	36
Lotte Goslar at The Liberated Theater	37
A Propos Aging. Sketch by Lotte Goslar	48
Program for the Columbia University 4-Star Dance Series	53
On Tour: Road Signs. Sketches by Lotte Goslar	58–63
Lotte Goslar in *Little Heap of Misery*	69
Ted Shawn, Lotte Goslar and Thomas Leabhart at Jacob's Pillow	73
Lotte and her husband Bill: the first new car	76
Lotte backstage with Charles Laughton, Elsa Lanchester, Bill Seehaus and Mrs. Cecil B. DeMille	79
Lotte in rehearsal for *Fairy Godmother*	83
Extract from the film animation of *Fairy Godmother*	83
Cats I've met	87
Mooky	92
Circus Scene. Sketch by Lotte Goslar	97
Lotte Goslar performing *So What?*	100
Bertolt Brecht and Lotte Goslar discussing his *Galileo*	100
From *Circus Scene*	103
The Lion from *Circus Scene*	105
Lotte Goslar in *Conversation with an Ant*	112
Hans and Ute Sahl	120

Solos created and danced by Lotte Goslar
   Intoxication   126
   The Life of a Flower   127
   Grande Tristesse   128
   Midnight Show   129
   Grandma Always Danced   130–132
   A Guardian Angel   133
   Cheap Clown – Not Wanted   134
   Gift Wrapped   135

The Company
   Lotte Goslar and The Company in *Greetings*   138
   The Pantomime Circus in *Pink Waltzes*   139
   Lou Zeldis and Kathleen Carlin in *Infatuation*   140
   Lotte Goslar, Lance Westergard and Algul Gamma
      in *Hello! Hello?*   141
   Lotte Goslar's *Talent Show*   142
   Lotte Goslar and Jess Meeker in *Liebestraum*   143

Bertolt Brecht's *Aus dem Zirkusleben (From Life in the Circus)*   146
Letter to Lotte Goslar from Bertolt Brecht, Berlin,
   12 March 1951   148
Lotte Goslar with Joseph Papp and Bernard Gersten   155
Ah, to live in the country! Sketch by Lotte Goslar   162
Lotte Goslar at home in Connecticut   163
Self-portrait with pear. Sketch by Lotte Goslar   164

Lotte Goslar – For Instance, a Clown

by Horst Koegler

Her name is Goslar, but she was born in Dresden. She wanted to become a dancer and studied with Palucca, but she became a mime and a clown and created for herself her own form that she called "Pantomime Circus." Clive Barnes, once the all-powerful theater critic of *The New York Times*, took the easy way out and called her simply "divine."

However, sitting opposite her and hearing her talk, I am left with anything but a divine impression. Around her eyes it can gleam quite devilishly. The real Goslar can probably be found halfway between God and the devil because she is totally of this, our world. Something sunny radiates from her. Not the sun that burns, but a sun that warms beneficially, filtered through a humanity that has experienced and lived through much and has become wise, and whose basic substance is kindness.

There is something of Verdi's Falstaffian "All is jest on earth" about her, a heart-warming humor, to whom nothing human is unknown. Of course, behind the ability to laugh about the foolishness of this world stands also the knowledge of the dark sides of today's human existence. That in essence gives the depth to her very personal, very Saxo-American humor. Exactly because she is looking at the bottom of everything, she cannot take it all so terribly seriously any longer.

She is a tireless teller of tales – especially on stage. But she not only tells of human beings, she also tells of music, of animals, of trees and of things carelessly thrown away. Her funny stories are never only funny; her thoughtful tales never only serious. What gives her pieces the individual flavor is the balance between the amusing and the reflective. It is a form of pantomime, whose parents are named Dance and Music. She is light and gossamer, and her points hit with unerring precision.

Sometime she will have to write down the story of her life. And then, finally, we will learn something more precise about her impressions of the Berlin of the golden twenties and the not so golden early thirties. And about her decision to leave Germany in 1933, not because she had to, but "because of a natural aversion to the Nazis." And about her touring with Erika Mann's cabaret The Peppermill, starting in Switzerland and criss-crossing through Europe. And about her arrival in 1939 in

America, where she subsequently collaborated with Brecht and Laughton on *Galileo Galilei* in Hollywood, before she made herself independent and, in 1954, founded her Pantomime Circus.

In an interview some years ago she expressed what she saw as her duty: "To be funny, that is, to bring joy, one has to be capable of experiencing at least a measure of joy oneself. Not happiness necessarily – that might be asking too much – but joy. And I believe that there are a few good reasons for that. Love, friendship, decency, courage still exist. Even today. One cannot deny them altogether. Just as it would be invalid to deny the vast supplies of hate, greed and hypocrisy. It still makes sense to pursue the one and fight the other. But to do that one must be an optimist. For instance, a clown."

Emigration

Emigration. Oil painting by Arthur Kaufmann. Lotte Goslar is directly under the Stars and Stripes. Courtesy of Städtisches Museum, Mülheim an der Ruhr, Germany

Key

1. Berthold Viertel, writer, stage director
2. Fritz Lang, film director
3. Günther Anders, writer
4. Ernst Toch, composer
5. Ernst Bloch, philosopher
6. Arthur Kaufmann, painter
7. Elisabeth Musset-Kaufmann, psychologist
8. Max Wertheimer, psychologist
9. Emanuel Feuermann, cellist
10. Arnold Schönberg, composer
11. George Grosz, painter
12. Joseph Floch, painter
13. Heinrich Mann, writer
14. Paul Zucker, art historian, architect
15. Luise Rainer, actress
16. Ulrich Friedemann, physician, bacteriologist
17. Otto Klemperer, conductor
18. Paul Tillich, theologian
19. Arnold Zweig, writer
20. William Stern, psychologist
21. Ferdinand Bruckner writer
22. Albert Einstein, physicist
23. Klaus Mann, writer
24. Thomas Mann, writer
25. Erika Mann, writer
26. Ludwig Renn, writer
27. Curt Valentin, art dealer
28. Hans Jelinek, graphic artist
29. Bruno Frank, writer
30. Erwin Piscator, stage director
31. Lotte Goslar, dancer
32. Oskar Maria Graf, writer
33. Benedikt Fred Dolbin, artist
34. Kurt Goldstein, physician, neurologist
35. Kurt Weill, composer
36. Max Reinhardt, stage director
37. Helene Thimig, actress
38. Ernst Toller, writer

MOVEMENT THEATRE INTERNATIONAL
Michael A. Pedretti, director
presents

LOTTE GOSLAR's PANTOMIME CIRCUS
in
SCENES AND DANCES

with
Kathleen Carlin, Mary Gambardella, Stephanie Godino, Lotte Goslar, Charles Haack, Ken Kempe, Lance Westergard, Musical Director and Pianist: **Richard Mercier**, Lighting Designer and Stage Manager: **Alex Koziara**

Program:

Greetings	All
Bounces	Company
Heap of Misery	Lotte
Collectors Items I	Charles, Lance, Stephanie, Mary
Collectors Items II	Charles, Lance, Kathleen, Mary
A Walk in the Woods	Stephanie
Love (from *Human Relations*)	Charles, Kathleen, Ken
Variations on an Old Theme	Mary, Lance
Splendor in the Grass	Charles, Stephanie, Kathleen, Lance
Portrait of my Mother	Lotte
Valse Very Triste	All

-There will be a 10 minute intermission-

La Donna de Dondolo (or: *The Swinging Beauty*) A Ballet	
Three Evils	Lance, Mary, Ken
A Nun	Stephanie
A Fairy Godmother	Lotte
A Shepherd	Charles
La Donna	Kathleen
An Innkeeper	Ken
Two Grape Stompers	Mary, Stephanie
A Grape Picker	Lance
A Sheriff	Ken
A Messenger	Lance
Liebestraum	Richard, Lotte
It Starts with a Step	Lance
A Composer	Ken
Auf Wiedersehn	
The Son	Charles
Mama	Lotte
Two Daughters	Kathleen, Stephanie
The Sweetheart	Mary
Daddy	Lance
Young Farmhand	Ken
Talent Show	Kathleen, Stephanie, Mary
All the Kings Men	Ken, Charles, Lance
Life of a Flower	Lotte
Pink Waltzes	Company

Program subject to change
Choreography and Costume design: Lotte Goslar
Costumes executed in New York and Amsterdam, Holland.
Lotte Goslar gratefully acknowledges the support of the National Endowment for the Arts, the N.Y. State Council on the Arts, and the assistance of the DIA Art Foundation, N.Y.

Program for Lotte Goslar's Pantomime Circus

An Explanation

Lotte Goslar's Pantomime Circus Foundation, Inc.

Lotte Goslar's Pantomime Circus is a unique and very personal blend of dance, theater and pantomime with the focus on dance. The title, first used by the European press, is simply an attempt to describe the scope of the show and its appeal to a wide range of ages. Actually it is neither a circus nor a mime show in the sense of the white-faced *mime pure*. But the spirit of the circus is there. It is a colorful and rousing show that runs number after number without pauses except for one intermission. Each of the twenty sections is a world in itself with its own distinct atmosphere. There is fun and clowning and music throughout. But the elements of comedy are used deceptively because a much more serious viewpoint runs through it all. It is a *Comédie Humaine* and much of the program is concerned with the human condition in our time. What people do to each other, good or bad – what they dream of, hope for, pretend, love or fear – is shown in terms of seemingly lighthearted or hilarious fun. A few serious numbers, pure dances and fantasy pieces complement different editions of the Pantomime Circus.

The company consists of six highly skilled dancers (trained in ballet, modern dance, some acrobatics and Lotte Goslar's special brand of subtle, seemingly natural dance-mime), a "live" concert pianist, a stage manager, and of course Lotte Goslar, who created all the adult and children's programs. Her aim is to offer entertainment with a deeper meaning, a kaleidoscope of life which is optimistic in spite of being critical – a true evening in the theater.

Members of the company (with dates of joining) have recently included: Kathleen Carlin, 1968 (except 1974–78); Gene French, 1980 (died in 1993); Mary Gambardella, 1990; Stephanie Godino, 1980; Charles Haak, 1977; Richard Mercier (Music Director), 1974; and Lance Westergard, 1968 (except 1974–81).

How Sweet It Is

How sweet it is – success, applause, good reviews – friends coming backstage to tell you you've never been better – strangers saying "Where have you been all my life?" In spite of the fact that you know full well it could not have been all that good, how sweet it is...

My biggest success came in Chicago, where I performed with the great actors George Voskovec and Jan Werich (refugees like myself) in a special program for their Czechoslovakian compatriots. I had danced some years before in their fabulous Liberated Theater in Prague, and now I was to join them again on that special evening, performing some solo pieces. I had just finished my first number, a short curtain-raiser, when an avalanche of applause broke loose such as I had never experienced before. Not three curtain calls, not five, not ten, but at least 15! At that time I always took my bows in character, and pretty soon I was out of fresh ideas. I could not see the audience because the spotlights were shining directly, blindingly into my eyes. Finally I went as far to the front of the stage as possible to get a look at this extraordinary crowd. And I saw that they all had risen to their feet in a standing ovation, but with their backs toward me. What had happened? Eduard Beneš, the president-in-exile, their great hero, had arrived and was standing in the balcony. All the applause had been for him! And I had taken my bows – in character – toward their behinds!!! The only one who had seen me making a fool of myself was Beneš. I hope.

I also fondly remember our première in Amsterdam. During a hectic performance three little boys kept coming backstage, pestering us for autographs. Of course we gave them, pretending only a little annoyance. After all, even if they were only kids, here was a new generation, our future audience, clamoring for us. Until we discovered that the same little boys came back several times, and finally we found out that they were selling our autographs on the street – for five cents!

How far does one go to keep success rolling? Well, in Italy, there was an insane manager who had publicized us as "Balletto di Hollywood." As a result, the square in front of every theater was filled with young men waiting for hours to see the glamorous stars arrive. I simply asked Rosalind de Mille, one of my beautiful young dancers, to step out of the car first as if she were me; I would follow her carrying suitcases as if I were her dresser. It worked. There was a howl of appreciation for her. And everyone was happy.

And what about this kind of success? Again, in Holland, we had been on TV and were utterly disgusted with the result. The next morning as I was walking on Calverstraat, a man on the other side of the street called over to me: "I saw you on TV last night. Wow!" "Oh," I said, "I thought it was terrible." "Right" he said.

To be copied is supposed to be the ultimate praise. In Switzerland a young mime travelled around doing an entire program of my numbers without mentioning my name. I thought that was a bit much, so when I met him, I told him so. He could not understand my concern. "But Lotte," he said, "I'm a communist. Your work is needed by the masses. I'm giving them what they need. You are trying to deprive them." He had a point!

My favorite "success" story happened in New York years ago when things were especially rough for me: no engagements; no manager; no students; no money. Nevertheless, I managed, as always, to live in a place that could serve as a studio, so at least I could dance. The building was old, the elevator rickety, the elevator man a little shriveled guy who looked like a yodel sounds. On one of the most dismal, cold, rainy days he brought me up to my third floor studio. During the slow, slow ride to the first floor, he took a long look at me with his little beady eyes and said: "You know, Miss Gosling, you are not beautiful." That was all I needed on this gray morning. "All right," I said, "I know." Silence. Between the first and second floors he looked at me again, long and slow. "You aren't even pretty," he said. "Okay," I answered, "rub it in." He opened the door to the third floor for me, and as I was trotting down the hallway, cold and dejected, I heard him yell: "But you've got what it takes!"

Another much more delicate memory of that sort is of a time many years ago when I was engaged to perform in a summer show near New York. It was a mixed program of several New York artists, and we all arrived a few days before the first performance. So there was time to get acquainted. Among many others there was a young pianist, the accompanist for Paul Draper, who obviously liked me. We went for walks, or he played for me, beautifully, from his concert repertoire. And he would always look at me with shy, warm eyes. Never more. The day of the performance came, and I was standing in the wings ready to go on in my first number called "Old Clown." I had totally disguised myself to portray the character. My body was completely covered with an outrageous potato sack; huge shoes and gloves hid my feet and hands;

my hair was under a wig; my nose under a big bulb; and makeup covered every bit of my own skin. There was no "me" to be seen, but only an old, old, overstuffed clown. The young man was standing next to me. I felt his warm, shy look on me and this is what he whispered into the huge plastic ear that covered my own: "You are lovely."

First Memories

I was born in Dresden, Germany, into a family that could be called bourgeois, but that was amazingly liberal in its attitude toward life in general. Therefore, as I grew up after World War I, I never had to overcome any prejudices about people who were different from myself, whether in race, or religion, or life-style or anything else. My father was a "Procurist" at a large bank. (Later my mother told us that – just before his death – he had been promoted to be a Director, but that the letter with the announcement arrived after he died. So he never knew.)

What do I remember about my father? That he was tall and very pale and very serious and that he had a big coal-black beard, all of which created a certain awe in my feelings toward him. But I know he was a deeply loving and understanding man. Because of his work we hardly saw him during the week, but on weekends he was totally the family man, leading us on many wonderful trips into the forests and mountains surrounding Dresden, usually ending up with him carrying me home on his back, because I had fallen asleep. He also was an outstanding amateur musician. Every night, after his dinner, he played the piano or his cello, and my brothers and I would fall asleep to the sounds of Schubert, Beethoven, Mozart or Scarlatti, of course not knowing who the composers were. I remember once being so inspired by my father's piano rendition of the opening of Beethoven's Fifth Symphony that I got out of bed and danced the entire piece using the only steps I knew at that time: heel, toe, 1, 2, 3; heel, toe, 1, 2, 3; repeating them over and over again and in all the variations from legato to furioso. My father also took us sometimes – one at a time – to Philharmonic concerts. I recall how infinitely bored I was at that age, when they played Johann Sebastian Bach. And how upset

Right heel, right toe, etc.

when during a museum visit, I could find neither dogs nor cats in any of the celestial paintings. "Don't they go to heaven" I wondered?

I am puzzled that I recall very little about my three brothers from that early time. I was the youngest and sort of an afterthought. In a hazy way I remember that they teased me a lot, but they also protected me in a big-brother fashion. They even let me play football with them since I was sort of a tomboy. In general I think we liked each other, but not much detail has remained in my memory. Strange!

Both my parents supported every bit of talent that tried to sprout into the open, even if it didn't amount to more than a passing interest. They always encouraged my rather lively fantasies, and I am sure they would have loved to see me become a dancer. But they did not live long enough.

The focus of my early life was definitely my mother. I wanted to be like her, and I remember once hammering at my feet, so I could have bunions like hers. There were so many things she said that have followed me all through life. "Every day is Sunday," was one, which of course meant that I could wear my prettiest dresses all through the week. "When something bad happens to you – like you break or lose something – tell yourself it's bad, but ask yourself: Is it *that* bad? Most of the time you'll find it isn't." Or the games we played together like "Fun without Money" at the time when we didn't have any, or "Dominos with Cheating," which was usually the high point at the end of the game that we all had been waiting for.

When I was about three years old we had a cat. I complained to my mother that because she was so little, she could see the chairs and tables only from underneath, where they were unfinished and really didn't look nice. So my mother got a big box of colored crayons and she and I drew pictures of birds and flowers and mice and sunshine on the bottoms of the furniture for pussycat (who of course couldn't have cared less). She also invented a secret magic place for me, right there in our living room. As she peeked with me through an imaginary curtain, a fantastic world would open up where anything was possible. I found out right then and there that I didn't have to own everything I liked. In my imagination I could go much further than in reality.

In those early years I was always afraid of losing my mother. If she was only going across the street to a store, I would sit in the window following her with my eyes until she disappeared, being convinced that I would never ever see her again. No assurance from any grown-up that of course I would, could stop an endless flood of tears. Also sometimes at night, I would get up secretly and tiptoe into my parents' bedroom. There I would stand next to my mother, listening to find out

My mother

whether she was still breathing. Since she was a very soundless sleeper, it sometimes took quite a while before I was convinced that I had not lost her.

Once – maybe I was about six years old – my mother took me with her to the bank in the center of town to visit my father. We went by streetcar, but got off one stop too early. To make up for the loss of time, my mother decided to take a short cut, a narrow crooked, cobblestoned street that seemed empty. She didn't know that this was the red-light district of Dresden. No sooner had we entered, than a storm broke loose. Like a Fellini film, out of every door and every window appeared strange women with painted faces, half naked, shaking their fists and screaming threats and abuses: "You dirty, filthy pig! Dragging an innocent little child through this gutter! Aren't you ashamed?" I still see myself hanging on to my sweet mother's hand as she was running for her life – our lives – through the rest of the, thank God, short street, followed by a swarm of yelping hyenas. Of course I didn't know what it all meant, but I still can see the chalk-white faces with the screaming, blood-red lips and the wet cobblestones. It was very frightening, and from then on I knew that outside of our nest at home, there was another unknown and very dangerous world.

Of all the memories I have of my earliest life, two are most unforgettable. They also could not be more different from one another. One, although almost nothing, is, I think, beautiful. It was a sunny day and I had come from the kitchen where I had found a basket with ripe plums. I loved to eat them, but was not supposed to. Nevertheless, I had taken two and was gleefully holding one in each hand. As I was entering the next room, I saw my mother coming toward me. Behind her was an open window with light curtains softly moving. The sun made her hair look golden and she smiled. The keys she wore on a ribbon around her waist were tinkling and life was wonderful. What I remember so much about that nothingness is a great deal. I had done something wrong. I knew it and I expected my mother to be angry. But no. She smiled, and the sun was shining. An absolute nothingness, but so very much: love, protection, mother, nest, the smell of ripe plums, mischief and forgiveness. Everything.

The other memory. I was about three years old. My six-year-old brother Walter had died, but I was not aware of it. In my memory my father carries me on his arm. His face is white as chalk, framed by his black beard. He brings me into the room where my brother is lying in his coffin. I think he is asleep. When my father asks me to say Goodbye, I lean over and reach for Walter's hand. It is ice cold, and I drop it. It flops down, dangling. And suddenly I know what death is.

In spite of all the love I received from my parents, there was a strange layer of darkness over my childhood that I cannot easily explain. I remember seeing a lot of little tragedies, observing every bug that had been stepped on, every flower that had been thrown away. For a whole year I collected things that were of no use to anyone – a bent nail, a short piece of string, half a hairpin – and put them on a shelf where my toys had been before. I don't know what made me finally stop that strange behavior. Of course we did not have as many toys as today's children. And I am glad about that. All through my childhood I had one doll whom I really loved. And two small stuffed animals. That was all, but it was plenty.

Strangely enough, I was sometimes painfully shy. The only reason I can think of is that, after my father's early death, we were suddenly

The toddler

poor and had to accept a lot of charity. I was a fiercely proud child and could not face taking hand-outs. I withdrew more and more, and it was dance, I believe, and some unexplainable bursts of inner joy that kept me from becoming morose. At the same time, in spite of all that shyness, I had become a show-off of sorts. It seems I needed something grandiose to happen in my not very glamorous life, and I remember a few attempts in that direction. I especially wanted to bring my mother some fabulous presents. Not just something little, but grand! So one day I decided that I would buy her a beautiful bouquet of flowers. Except of course I had no money whatsoever. But that did not stop me. On my way to school I had quite often passed a very elegant flower shop and had seen in its windows the most gorgeous displays: vases filled with red tulips, yellow roses, blue hyacinths, white carnations. I knew my mother loved them, and I was going to give them to her. So one day on my way home from school, I entered the shop. A nice young lady asked me what she could do for me, and after lying that it was for my mother's birthday, I directed her to assemble a huge bouquet, picking out one of each of the most beautiful (and expensive!) flowers. All the time my heart pounded from fear and excitement. Did I want special birthday wrapping? Yes, of course, I said. She went to the back of the store to finish the bouquet, and at that moment it suddenly dawned on me what a horrendous situation I had gotten myself into, and I ran out of the store. I made it home and nothing ever happened about that fraud. But from that day on I had to take a much longer way to school because I did not dare pass that shop again. That should have taught me a lesson.

And in a way it did. I now decided to earn some money so I could legitimately buy something beautiful for my mother. I had heard that the druggist on our corner sometimes bought herbs, like peppermint or chamomile, from people he knew. Also hirtentaschel (shepherds pockets), an herb that as a tea was used for inhalation. I knew where to find it. Lots of it. And since the druggist offered me ten pennies a pound, and I certainly could bring him at least twenty pounds, I knew I would earn two marks for sure, at that time an unbelievable fortune. What could I buy with it for my mother? Maybe a blouse. Maybe a hat. Maybe a beautiful silken scarf? And what if I could bring in twice as much of the hirtentaschel? I would have four marks to spend! Oh my God! There was absolutely no limit. Once in a while my mother used to visit her sister in Berlin, sometimes for as long as a whole week. So all I had to do was wait for one of those times. And luckily it didn't take long. The morning after she had left, at the crack of dawn, I took off on my bike with two rucksacks on the handlebars. And sure enough, all along the banks of the river Elbe, the golden hirtentaschel was ablaze. But – I was not the only one there. A whole gang of stray dogs had assembled for their morning rendez-vous, not only playing and fighting, but also watering the precious herbs. I went on to find another spot, and finally, although it had started raining heavily, I made it back to the drugstore. The man put my bags on the scale: almost thirty pounds! But then, opening them, he said, "My dear child, they are very wet. You'll have to dry them first before I can buy them." What could I do? I went home to spread my loot on the floor of our attic. Every day for the next three days I climbed up to check on the dryness, and on the fourth day I decided that everything was perfect. Back to the drugstore I biked with my bags, up on the scale they went, and my glorious thirty pounds had shrunk to something like five. And that was not all. "Dear child," the druggist said, "you have to cut off the stems before I can buy them." Hirtentaschel is all stem, long, tough and vicious stem, and what you use are the tiny seeds that dangle on spindly threads on top. They weigh almost nothing, and with all the handling most had come off anyway. Well, what do you think happened? I've always been quite stubborn when I believed in something. I went home. I cut all the stems off. I went back to the drugstore. My hirtentaschel was down to half a pound, and I got five cents. I don't remember what I bought for my mother, but I must have bought her something. Maybe a cookie or a short ribbon. But I went to a different store. For nothing in the world would have made me bring my business to that druggist.

Before my father died, we always had a live-in maid, which in our house meant they were part of the family, not "servants." They almost always were called Marie and usually they were with us not longer than a year. For a special reason. Apparently my mother could not bear the thought that these lovely young girls would grow up to become old spinsters. So she always tried – and successfully! – to find them a good husband. Which also meant that every year or so, she had to teach another Marie the intricacies of the job. But why were they always called Marie? They usually came from large families with many daughters and cousins and nieces, and since they had been very happy under my mother's guidance, their families used to implore my parents, once the wedding bells were ringing, to engage another of their offspring. Marie was a very common name at that time and it just so happened that we usually ended up with one. After my father died, however, we could not afford another Marie.

But I do remember a great benefit that came from the last one who had been with us. She now was married to a baker in a small village not far from Dresden, and they invited us for an afternoon of "Kaffee und Kuchen" in the country. This was in the middle of the worst famine in Germany, but they were of course much better off than we who lived in a big city. They had a cow and a pig and chickens. So my mother and we three children were looking forward to a feast. As Mariechen was milking the cow and making the coffee, her husband showed us around his place including the larder where he let us have a peek at a large plate brimming with cream puffs he had baked for us. This was to be a thank-you celebration. We couldn't believe our eyes. But when Marie went to the larder to bring in the cream puffs, there were none on the plate. Where were they? What had happened? My brother Erich, the one who never in his entire life had taken, stolen or otherwise criminally acquired anything that didn't belong to him, had been possessed by the devil and eaten them all. Every single one. Not my other brother Hans nor myself, whom one could not always totally trust when a temptation was too strong to resist, but Erich, the good son, the proper, respectable, decent Erich! After seeing the plate of cream puffs, he simply could not leave it alone. Like a sleepwalker he was pulled by mysterious forces back to the larder. He couldn't help himself. And I believe that all the assembled grown-ups felt the same way. "He couldn't help himself."

At home in those years everything we ate seemed to be made from turnips: coffee, marmalade, bread, meatballs. Everything. And we developed quite some cunning imagination to make the foods taste different from each other. Luckily we still had several leftover spices from better days. Also, once in a great while we were able to buy a small amount of some sinister-looking ground meat, and those were the days when we made "Schiebewurst." Schiebewurst, pronounced Scheebewurst and meaning Push sausage, was a concoction of about eighty per cent turnip and twenty per cent meat, plus several heaping tablespoons of salami spices to kill the taste of the turnips. We considered this event our red letter day, and all of us were eager to make it last as long as possible. So this is what we devised: we each got one slice of Schiebewurst which we put on the edge of our turnip bread close to our nose, and as our lips advanced on the bread, we pushed the sausage along ahead of the nose, so that when we had finished the bread, we still had the Schiebewurst to transfer to the next piece of bread – if there was one.

Palucca

My mother used to tell me that I started dancing in the cradle. I would throw myself up in the air, turn over, plunge down and smile. Thinking back to my childhood now, I see myself always "moving." In the hallway of our home I secretly "danced." Running back and forth between the huge armoires and swinging my mother's gauzy handkerchief, I believed myself to be a fairy or a lovely nymph. Nobody was allowed to see me though. Anybody opening a door made me disappear into the darkest corner. "Puss in Boots" at a Christmas show was the great and for a long time the only theater experience I had. Unforgettable how Puss kicked his leg high up in the air, hitting the king's nose. My first encounter with foolhardy audacity. My secret imagination grew into the direction: clown and fairy tale.

And then one day in school the great shock! At some celebration two older students danced a gymnastic étude. Somebody told me that they had been taking classes with Palucca. Palucca? Who was Palucca? I had never seen her, but I had heard that she had been a member of Mary Wigman's company until she left that group and made herself independent. And Mary Wigman of course was the high priestess of modern dance in Germany, comparable to Martha Graham in America. Suddenly, with tremendous impact, the up-to-now so beloved fairy tale panorama was torn open. An utterly new world confronted me. *Modern Dance*! I hadn't even known it existed. Plain, simple, unadorned. No gossamer veils, no decorations, no little bells. Instead, something like leotards, one bright blue, one shining yellow. Strong colors, simple shapes. The movements didn't tell stories; they were movements for movement's sake. The only thing that connected this new world with my former one was the same exhilaration, this joy of dancing, that – it seemed a thousand years ago – had made me chase as a lovely nymph through the hallway at home. There was only one way out: Palucca. I had to study with her. Nothing could stop me. An aunt paid for a short beginners' course, not with Palucca but at the Wigman school. I don't remember the reason for that, but at least it was "modern" dance. I was totally obsessed. I ate, slept, dreamed, bicycled modern dance. Without any money (which meant without music; I couldn't afford a pianist or even records), I invented my first dance: "In the Green Light," a rather lugubrious, deadly serious affair. Something was clearly wrong. Where on earth was the joy of dancing? In the beginners' class I had hardly any contact with Wigman. Her world remained mysterious to me, and her tremendous power did not touch me.

That's when I met Palucca. After much hesitation, I finally found the courage to ask her for a scholarship. She told me to come to her studio. In the much too long Lodencoat inherited from my very tall father and wearing his felt hat that looked like a pancake on me, I appeared at the "Bürgerwiese." Someone led me into her studio. My God! White walls, a huge black Blüthner grand piano and behind it a painting by Mondrian: fields of primary colors, nothing else. This – I knew instinctively and immediately – this is my world!

And then: a young girl enters, somehow boyish, with a strange face like a sculpture that hasn't been finished. This is Palucca: High forehead, audacious nose – very simple and totally relaxed. I am dancing for her. "In Green Light" of course. What else? That's all I have. Half way into the number, I stop and run crying from the studio. Because suddenly it has dawned on me that I am in the presence of a great artist. How unbelievably awful and pretentious all that nonsense is, that I had dared to show to her. She had not said a word, but had watched with interest. She followed me to the dressing room, was friendly and encouraging and said that she would call me. I ran home, deep in the dumps, and gave up all hope. Never before had I felt so worthless. Why do I tell all of this? Because it became the big turning point in my life, my first encounter with real greatness. Through her – Palucca's – presence alone, I suddenly knew, as clearly as light, what was true and what was fake.

Miracle after miracle! She did call me, and very soon, almost without training, she took me into her first company. Later she told me that precisely in my unfinished and somewhat confused condition she had discovered a natural talent.

Now a most wonderful time started. I was determined to live up to the qualities of the much better members of the company. And as soon as possible. I rehearsed and rehearsed and rehearsed from morning till midnight. Added to this came the big event; I saw Palucca herself dance. Not only on stage, but also improvising at her studio. Everything I could only guess before became reality.

Anyone who has never seen Palucca dance cannot even imagine her. To someone who does not know what a storm is or a sunset or the ocean, it is impossible to explain what it is all about. So basic, elementary is what she does. Again and again, when I saw her dance, I asked myself: Why can I not be so simple? People much more qualified have written about the lonely greatness of Palucca. For me it was even more; it was the confirmation of everything I was striving for. Everything that was important and valuable to me came together in this incredible artist.

And now something very strange happened – although seen from the distance, it was exactly what was to be expected. The more I tried to learn Palucca's style, the more I turned away from it. In spite of my unlimited admiration for her, this was not my language. Once more – as before at home – I started secretly to design my own dances. I was amazed. What I loved about Palucca's art was the abstraction; what came out of me was foolishness, clownerie, theater. I was bewildered, but couldn't stop. How she discovered my dilemma, how she tried to understand me, although I did not make it easy, and how she helped me bring my first attempts to an audience – all of that was the culmination of an impatient growing time. Only later did I fully realize how great a guiding spirit she was. Not to be like her, but to be as true as she in my own way, that was the great goal.

Since my emigration we have not seen each other for a long, long time. But from year to year it becomes clearer and clearer to me how much she has given me through her own great example: the courage to be myself and the way to simplicity. And much, much more.

Postscript 1990: We finally, in October 1990, met again. She is the same. Of course we both are older. But she has retained the same luminous quality, generous, wise and witty. And, yes, the same charm, and the same eternal youthfulness. How lucky her students are!

Postscript 1993: Palucca died in January 1993 in Dresden.

So Much Luck (I)

All through my life I have had an unusual amount of luck. It started right in the beginning of my professional life when I got an engagement from the prestigious "Volksbühne" theater in Berlin to share a program with two other up-and-coming young dancers. Until that time I had performed only in Palucca's concerts. This was my first chance to be on my own. With seven solos!

During that period I lived close to Palucca in the ballroom of two titled spinster ladies who had fallen on hard times and rented out most of their elegant villa. The place was ideal for dancing, which was all I cared about. There were four very tall mirrors, one in each corner, two of them facing each other across the room. My couch was placed in front of one of them, so that when I was lying in bed, I could see myself reflected many times, getting smaller and smaller and smaller. And that was also true for the candle which was my only light, and which created a rather spooky aura. Miraculously the ladies had left a rickety upright piano and someone had given me a phonograph, one of those old-fashioned machines, wind-up of course, which often did not make it to the end of a piece. I was in heaven! When not rehearsing with Palucca or teaching in her school, I was all by myself, and I danced and I danced and I danced. There was also a small iron stove on which I cooked my meals. They consisted mainly of spinach, tomatoes and cocoa, that were not only cheap, but healthy. Since I had only one pot, I remember frequently drinking my cocoa with some nutritious spinach leaves in it.

Soon Palucca started taking me along on her solo tours to do the same things that she had done for Mary Wigman: to beat the drum and other percussion instruments. "An der Trommel Lotte Goslar" (on the drums L. G.) was added to the posters announcing Palucca's performances. She was a favorite of the "Bauhaus" and often danced there. I was always invited to stay at the homes of the professors. So the little girl from Dresden met them all intimately – Klee and Kandinsky and Moholy-Nagy and Gropius and Breuer and many more. Usually there was a festivity after Palucca's performance, a supper party or a social dance. Was I intimidated by these giants? Was I flustered by this high life? Not at all. In spite of my initial shyness I took for granted that I belonged. Quite cool, I felt at home.

In Dresden, in my studio I soon had my own circle of friends; my colleagues from Palucca's company and their pals, young artists, architects and students from the universities. Often after our rehearsals they came to my place. We all huddled together on the floor and on the single couch to listen to our idols, Duke Ellington and Louis Armstrong, on my decrepit record player. Sometimes we sipped some inexpensive wine we had mixed haphazardly out of some left-overs from the day before, making us feel very grownup but also very sick. Or we improvised wild tangos all across the huge studio. We were free and strong and happy. And sometimes after midnight we all went to one of the many "Artists Balls" for which Dresden was famous. We all dressed up in some wild costumes. My favorite disguise was "Femme Fatale" (for which one year I won first prize together with Otto Dix, who I think came as a goat). It was all outrageous. And *sooo* innocent! I was always hiding behind an invented character who did the flirting, not I. Obviously I was growing up into a world of make-believe and phantasy and I think it is typical, that the best of my disguises later became dances for the stage.

The performance at the Volksbühne in Berlin was a matinée and was scheduled for twelve noon. In order to the there in good time, I had to take a train from Dresden in the middle of the night. To leave the day before and stay in a hotel was totally out of the question. Of course I rehearsed until deep into the night, packed my two trunks – except for a few socks that were soiled from the rehearsal and needed washing/drying near the stove – and set the borrowed alarm clock for 2 a.m. AND OVERSLEPT! This was in the middle of winter, and it had snowed heavily. I knew I could not possibly make it to the station on time. I had planned on about half an hour to walk to the train (of course I could not afford a taxi), and now it was exactly the time the train was scheduled to depart. I knew beyond any doubt that I did not have the slightest chance, but in a panic, I threw the still-damp socks into the trunks and ran, ran, slithered and stumbled to the station with the two heavy pieces of luggage, out of breath and desperate.

And what happened? My train was still there. It had snowed so heavily that all the trains were delayed. And no sooner had I fallen into my seat, then I heard the whistle, and off we went. I *had* made it. But if I hadn't, my entire life would have been different. Probably much more difficult, because that almost-missed performance was the biggest breakthrough I ever had. And here is some extra luck: Adolf Havlik, Palucca's brilliant pianist who was as crazy as all of us and who was to play for me, was at the station in Berlin when I arrived. Rich as he was (he really was) he took a taxi to the theater. And even more luck: I was last on the program – which gave me enough time to go to the theater's costume department and dry out my soggy socks.

Lotte Goslar as *Femme Fatale*. Photo: Otto Leib

Lotte Goslar as *The Disgruntled*. Photo: Constantine

The Disgruntled

The Disgruntled was the very first clown dance I ever made up. Although I usually think of my clown characters as "it," I shall, for simplicity's sake, use the pronoun "he." He was born in my studio in Dresden. I remember laughing myself silly when he appeared, but I doubted that anybody else would find him funny. I have no idea which corner of my fantasy he came from, but he became sort of my trademark for many years. I must have danced him more than a thousand times. He is an abstraction, a mood. Different audiences have seen him as a symbol of different concerns; some political ones as rebellion against whatever; children's groups as a sort of Poltergeist; and, I was told, that he became the pinup-picture of an English squadron in World War II. For me he was none of that in particular. He was just angry. Nonsense angry. I thought that nonsense-angry is funny. Stupid is funny. It can be laughed away.

There were some Turnabout audiences, the ones we used to call our Pasadena Ladies, who looked very much like the Disgruntled. They would come backstage and exclaim: "Miss Goslar! That Disgruntled! How did you think of a thing like that? It's uncanny!" I was sometimes tempted to tell them to look into a mirror. There was a certain similarity between them, except for the hats the ladies wore.

Many years later at the start of one of our European tours, I was interviewed in my hotel in Amsterdam, and was asked if I could tell a "human interest" story. For the occasion I had dressed rather elegantly. I was in the middle of my Disgruntled story miming those dear Pasadena ladies to the hilt, when I heard the click of a camera. So far so good. But next morning at breakfast on the front page of the biggest Dutch newspaper, there was my picture, in full regalia, but with the distorted Disgruntled face. No explanation whatsoever, simply saying, "Lotte Goslar Back in Europe."

A few years ago, at the 30th anniversary of my Pantomime Circus at the Joyce Theater in New York, I added *The Disgruntled* to the program, thinking that it would be interesting to the audience to see the very first clown dance I had created. But I don't believe he survived too well. He is from another time. So I'd better let him rest. Goodbye, Disgruntled!

Lotte Goslar in 1938

Lotte Goslar back in Europe. Drawing by Lotte Goslar

Up and Out

After the performance at the Volksbühne, my life changed considerably. I had been "discovered." In no time I was booked solid for almost a year, partly in concerts and often in Kabaretts, and even in nightclubs, which I did not like at all. The "Kabarett der Komiker," (the best variety show in Berlin, where you could see jugglers and acrobats but also some of the greatest stars of film and theater) held me over for many months, and Arthur Bernstein, the manager of Palucca and the newly discovered Walter Gieseking, signed me for a concert tour through municipal theaters. I was obviously "in." But the strange thing was that I was not even fully aware of my new status. Of course I read the reviews, and I must have seen my name in lights on the marquees, but none of that sank in. I was painfully shy, but at the same time self-assured and stubborn as far as my work was concerned: a strange mixture of naive and knowing, and certainly very immature. Sometimes people thought I was stuck-up when in reality I was simply scared. This was the most exciting time in the history of the Berlin Theater – a hotbed of creativity and frivolity: Max Reinhardt, Bertolt Brecht, Kurt Weill and Lotte Lenya, Valeska Gert, Friedrich Hollander's Cabaret "Tingel-Tangel," the night life and the whole avant garde. But unfortunately I shut myself off from it all. I had rented a room in some suburb and came into Berlin only for my performances. I did not take part at all in that rich turmoil. Later I realized what I had missed, and I've often regretted it.

In January 1933 I danced in the Skala, Berlin's biggest music hall, and signed a contract to return in January 1934. But in March of 1933 Hitler conquered Germany. I was dancing in Prague at the time and decided not to return. Actually, it was not a difficult decision. I had always felt more European than specifically German, and my life had been without roots anyway. So it was not the loss of my "Heimat" (fatherland) that concerned me, but the fact that many of my friends started to be harrassed – and soon persecuted – because of their political beliefs, or simply because they were Jewish or Gypsies or avant-garde artists. I felt I could not breathe in this country any longer. The director of the Skala tried to assure me that I had nothing to fear since I was not Jewish, and that by January 1934 Hitler would be gone anyway. He also warned me that the Skala would sue me if I broke my contract.

Needless to say, I could not have cared less. I made a hurried trip back to Berlin to pick up a few belongings from the room I had been renting. As I was saying good-bye to my rather bourgeois landladies, I heard marching music and saw a group of Brownshirts goose-stepping past the house. I will never forget the instant transformation of the two Fräulein, who a moment before had smiled sweetly at me and now were turning into wildly panting furies, moaning and gasping for breath and screaming in the tempo of the marchers: "Heil Hitler! Heil Hitler!" It was absolutely insane.

So now I returned to Prague, a newly born refugee. This beautiful city became very important to me for two reasons. It is there that I first met Hans Sahl, the best friend I ever had, and that in 1937 I joined the Liberated Theater of Voscovec and Werich, which became for me the greatest theater experience ever. The first meeting with Hans Sahl was typical of much that was to follow. Before he fled to Prague in 1933, he had created unusual interest in Berlin with his critiques and essays on the theater, on films and literature. In Prague he wrote for a small publication. They assigned him to interview me in the cabaret where I was appearing. He told me later that he had never seen me before, but had heard of me and had been intrigued by the tone of the comments in the Berlin press. He knew he would meet a dancer, of course. Maybe a delicate ballerina? When he arrived backstage, he was told that I had just gone out for a moment and that I would return presently. He waited in the hallway in front of my dressing room, and this is the way he remembers it all: there was the sound of a flushing toilet and with this accompaniment in the background, a door flew open and out came this:

Lotte Goslar as *The Wood Sprite*.
Photo: Constantine

Lotte Goslar as *The Wood Sprite*.
Photo: Constantine

An indelible introduction!

And with it our very special friendship, which has lasted through everything including our separate marriages. There were times when we saw each other often, and others when we did not meet for many months or even years because of long stretches of living in different parts of the world. Typical and unforgettable is one time when Hans lived in Switzerland and I, on my way from Holland to Czechoslovakia, was passing through Zurich. He came to the station, where I had to change trains, so we could at least get a glimpse of each other. But as I stepped down to the platform, my suitcase opened and everything – but everything – fell out. The five minutes that were allowed between trains were totally spent by both of us trying to collect the costumes, lipsticks, powder puffs and clowns noses that were scattered all over. Not even a short embrace, not even a kiss to say good-bye.

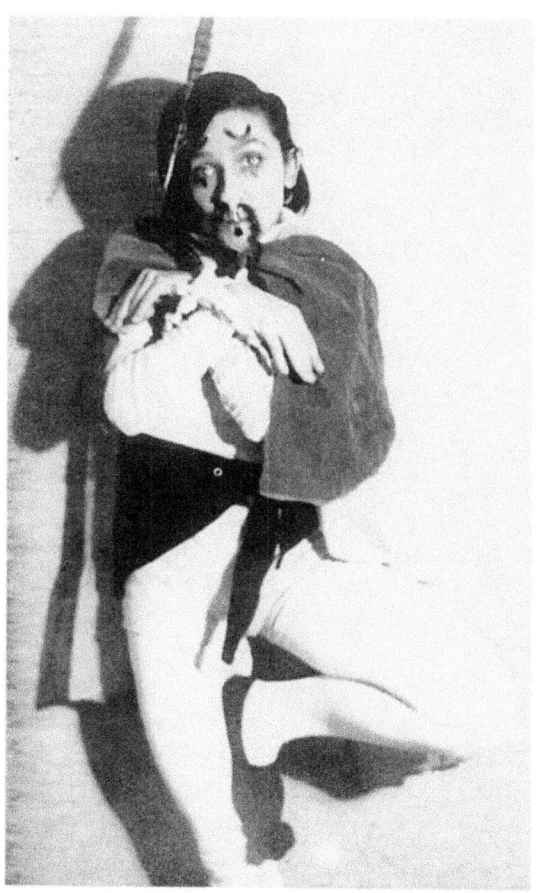

Lotte Goslar in *The Artist in Person*. Photo: Otto Leib

The Peppermill Theater

Outside Germany, the spawning ground of the literary and political cabaret, there soon developed a whole flood of anti-fascist theaters, a type of show that was not known in America: satirical, highly intellectual and at the same time, entertaining. One of them, the Ping-Pong in Amsterdam, engaged me for several months, and after that Erika Mann invited me to join her "Peppermill" in Zürich. I was to arrive two days before the premiere of their new show, so that I could see their current program to get an idea of what the Peppermill was all about. I was to dance the three numbers I had done on the big stages in Berlin. I arrived at their location, called "Der Hirsch," (The Stag) at noon, and I nearly collapsed when I saw the place. This was no theater and there was no stage! Instead there was a small room filled with tables and chairs for people to drink their beer and eat their bockwurst. At one end there was a tiny platform for a singer or two or for a comedian, provided that he or she didn't move too much, but certainly not for a dancer intending to leap from one wing to the other. And nobody was there to greet me and to tell me that, of course, I would not be expected to dance on this postage stamp. So I sat down and waited. And waited. And waited.

And after a long time a woman came from backstage who apparently was one of the cleaning women going home. A heavy-set workhorse. "Are you Goslar?" she said. "I'm Giehse." Now for anyone who does not know about Giehse, let me explain. Therese Giehse was – and not only in my book – one of the greatest actresses ever. I had heard of her, of course, but had never seen her. I could have died. This was the famous Giehse? No stage, no theater, and on top of it, this was supposed to be the great actress who had been one of the reasons why I had accepted the engagement? What on earth had I gotten myself into? Soon after this shock, Erika and the rest of the company arrived. And Erika had a special request. Sybille Schloss, their ingenue, had the flu and could not perform for the next two nights. Would I, Erika asked, replace her in just one sketch? Only one sentence, but the scene could not be done without that character. I swallowed my anger and said yes. The sketch was about a group of cackling gossips at a cocktail party, and I was to portray the friend of the hostess who arrives at the last minute and, seeing them, exclaims in disgust: "These are the stars? And I took a taxi!" Up to that day, I had never spoken on stage. But I was confident; of course I could do it. What happened? I entered, stumbled, fell down and said: "These are the taxis? And I took a star!" – remaining rooted on my behind, reasoning that the audience would think I crashed on purpose, if I didn't get up. The curtain fell, and I still remember Klaus Mann, who had seen it all from the audience, rushing backstage muttering: "It didn't happen! It can't have happened!" Erika, however, true to form, had the courage to ask me to do that sketch again the next day, and I, true to form, had the nerve, out of sheer pride and ambition, to repeat the performance. And of course I fell down again and said once more: "These are the taxis? And I took a star!" Again not getting up. Of course, no one from the Peppermill ever again asked me to utter a word on stage.

It was Charles Laughton – years later – who helped me to get totally over the fear of speaking on stage, with just one piece of sound advice. But more about that in another chapter. Something much more important happened that night: I saw Therese Giehse perform in her chansons and in several sketches. I was overwhelmed! And it is still hard for me to comprehend how I could ever have been so stupid and insensitive in my judgment when I first met her.

So, of course, I stayed with the Peppermill, and it became a very important time of my life. Between January '34 and September '35 I performed with the company all over Switzerland, Holland and Czechoslovakia, and also in Belgium and Luxemburg. The audiences were a dream. Everywhere they were a mixture of the anti-fascists of our guest countries and the refugees from Germany. After the shows we would often meet groups of them in the little restaurants where we ate our supper. Some of them were world famous, some not at all. We huddled at the same tables until deep into the night: a big brotherhood in countries we didn't even know. Are you a communist? Are you a socialist? Are you without politics? It didn't matter then. We had the same enemy. We were all friends. How idyllic this sounds! In reality we were close to the German border and the danger of kidnapping was real especially for Erika, whose tremendous courage and strength in endless battles with some reluctant civic authorities kept the Peppermill alive. One problem was that we were given only limited permits to stay and play in each country. We could return after a few days, but first we had to leave. The worst was that sometimes we had to produce "good conduct" certificates in order to receive our visas, and those we could only get from the German consulates. At that time the stamps in the passports always named the place of employment. So the word "Peppermill" was on every page, and it was only sheer luck that the clerks at the different consulates did not seem to notice. We could have been sent back "home." All the time we heard more and more about the atrocities in Germany, sometimes from some daring underground people who had crossed the borders. And more and more we were unsure about how much longer we would be tolerated by the countries we visited. But in spite of it all, our spirits were high. We were whistling in the dark. Of course, we were very lucky to be outside Hitler's Germany. Still, in many ways it was not easy to be an emigrant. In spite of meeting so many like-minded people, I have never been as lonely as during that time. It was impossible to build any lasting relationship when one forever had to leave again and say another of the many good-byes.

In 1935 in Zürich, where we played in a larger theater, the Peppermill was attacked by a big group of Swiss Nazis who had bought out the front part of the house. The leader happened to be the brother of one of Erika's best friends, who, being on our side, informed her immediately. This gave Erika enough time to fill the rest of the theater with our own sturdy friends who were willing to fight back if needed. It became an ugly and dangerous battle. Chairs, ripped apart, were used as weapons, and there was tear gas and shooting. In the end nobody was seriously hurt, but I think it is important to know that as a result the Peppermill was forbidden in Switzerland (and later in Holland). Not the Swiss Nazis, who had organized the coup, but the Peppermill. It showed how difficult it was to fight fascism even from outside Germany and how much more dangerous it must have been to oppose it from within.

The Liberated Theater

After the Swiss disaster, the Peppermill went on a Czechoslovakian tour for two months which included two weeks in Prague, the home of the famous Liberated Theater. It had been created a few years back by Jiři Voskovec and Jan Werich, two rebellious students at the University of Prague, as a satirical showcase with strong anti-fascist overtones and very much targeted against some of the professors. Voskovec and Werich immediately became the gods of the new generation of students, but they so angered the hierarchy of the university that they were told either to stop their performances or leave the institution. They left. And they started their own legitimate theater, the Osvobozeneho Divadla (The Liberated Theater), which not only became the toast of Prague and all of Czechoslovakia, but also was known all over Europe as the most exciting avant-garde theater of its time. As part of the Peppermill program in Prague, I was to dance a number called "The Artist in Person," a satire on the vanity of a self-important and very ridiculous would-be artist. No sooner had I started the dance, than thunderous, bellowing laughter came from the auditorium, which soon became a whole orchestration of screams and yellings and guffaws. It had started with one person, but it had infected the whole house by the time I was about half through my number. This one person was Jan Werich, who was sitting with Voskovec in the center of the theater, bobbing up and down, slapping his and his partner's thighs and snorting in agonized delight. Of course everybody now looked at Werich and not any more at the stage – and certainly not at me. And they all shrieked and laughed so loud that I could not hear my own music any longer and simply had to stop. I just stood there – helpless, before I vanished into the wings. Afterwards Werich came backstage and said, "Lottinka, you belong to us."

I joined the Liberated Theater after the Peppermill had finished the Czech tour and stayed with them almost a year for the run of "Balada z Hadrů" (Ballad of Rags). Except that when I joined them, they had changed to a smaller theater which they renamed Noviny Spoutaneho Divadla (The New Chained Theater) for a special reason: the owners of the building that housed their Liberated Theater turned out to be fervent Czech Nazis. In order to get rid of Voskovec and Werich they raised the rent so high that the two could not possibly afford it. Later, during the end of the run, they moved again to a larger house, and it became once more the Liberated Theater.

Although it is not easy, I will try to describe what their shows were like. Voskovec and Werich were an ideal team, although they were very different from one another. Werich looked like a mixture of Falstaff and Buddha. He was very tall and heavy, with a round face like a full moon, slit eyes and a slit mouth which he emphasized with his makeup. His whole personality, on stage and in real life, was lusty and rich and juicy. When he laughed, the walls trembled, and when he spoke he engulfed you with his humor. Voskovec was also tall, but slim and very beautiful. His humor was elegant and poetic, but with a poisonous edge to it. In a way they were modern reincarnations of the Pierrot and the Auguste of the Commedia del' Arte. I believe that Voskovec did most of the writing, but Werich added many of the hilarious improvisations on stage. The word "genius" is much overworked, I know, but it is the only way to describe Voskovec and Werich. They were way ahead of their time, and it was only recently when I saw the wonderful Canadian

Werich and Voskovec

Cirque du Soleil that I was reminded of some of their qualities. Like Balada z Hadrů, which was based on the life and writings of François Villon, all their plays were regular theater pieces with a regular cast and all the trimmings, conflicts and love interests of a regular comedy. In a way it was Voskovec and Werich's way of fooling their audience, of lulling them into the safe feeling of – this is just entertainment, nothing can go wrong. Until these two appeared and totally destroyed your safeguards. Their physical appearance was that of clowns, but clowns of a very fantastic kind. Everyone else in the play looked "normal," bourgeois, regular, unsurprising, but they were dressed in outlandish garb. They wore surrealistic makeup and strange hairpieces that made Werich even more the incarnation of cunning pseudo-stupidity and Voskovec even more the raconteur you'd better be careful of. First you saw them as part of the regular action, as observers, in the disguise of a night watchman and a street cleaner of the Middle Ages. But then, several times during the show, the stage was divided midway by a curtain that closed in front of the entire set and left only a bare and rather large forestage to be seen. Voskovec and Werich stepped through that curtain and now the real show started. Each of the four "interruptions" lasted from ten to twenty minutes. They were the wildest non-stop improvisations you can imagine. All of them were based on the current topical news, although seemingly induced by the world of François Villon. They danced, they sang, they juggled. They threw words at each other and played ball with them. Sometimes they broke up over each other's improvisations. What made it all even more wondrous was that their composer–conductor, Jaroslav Ježek, and his small combo improvised right along with them. It was – four times during the play – a feast of hilarity, madness and deeper meaning. Four times the midstage curtain also closed for the dances that I had choreographed mostly to music Ježek had written for me. Voskovec and Werich left me total freedom as long as the themes had some connection with the play. "Fille de Joie," "The Guardian Angel," "Young Mother," and "Intoxication" were some of the titles. In addition, on dark nights, Voskovec and Werich let me use the theater for my own concerts and Ježek's small orchestra played for me. A wonderful, wonderful creative time. Their generosity was unlimited.

    I wish it were possible to re-issue their productions, using the news of today. They would be very much of our time, although their own contributions would be hard to match. I assume that their impact had much to do with their being Czech. After all, this was the country that had created the legendary folk hero: the Good Soldier Schwejk.

    To be in Prague for a whole year and not to live out of trunks was, of course, heaven. It became a very creative time for me. The Czechs are

BALADA Z HADRŮ

Divadlo o prokletém básníkovi v 16 obrazech. – Napsali Voskovec a Werich – Hudbu složil J. Ježek – Režie J. Honzl – Balet L. Goslarová – Výprava B. Feuerstein – Kostýmy F. Zelenka – V citátech Villonových veršů použili autoři překladů O. Fischera – Balety L. Goslarové na hudbu různých autorů

Obraz 1. Pět set let

Kateřina	J. Švabíková
Zebračka	Molnárová
Nezaměstnaný	F. Filipovský
Nezaměstnaná	B. Waleská
Student	J. Plachta
Herec	B. Záhorský
Hlídač	J. Savrda

Obraz 2. Král a pirát

Purkmistr města Paříže	J. Plachta
François Villon, básník	B. Záhorský

Obraz 3. Srdce na dlani

Villon	B. Záhorský
Kateřina de Vausselles	J. Švabíková
Zahalená kráska	L. Goslarová

Tanec Lotte Goslarová

Obraz 4. Noc lásky

Purkmistr	J. Plachta
Kateřina	J. Švabíková
Filip Sermoise	F. Filipovský

Obraz 5. Čistý štít

Purkmistr	J. Plachta

Obraz 6. Pyká se a troubí

Georges, antoušek	J. Voskovec
Jehan, ponocný	J. Werich

Hej pane králi… Voskovec & Werich

Purkmistr	J. Plachta
Villon	B. Záhorský
Pařížský lid	

Obraz 7. Slovo dá slovo

Voskovec & Werich

Obraz 8. Vše kam patří

Šenkýřka	I. Lechnýřová
Filip	F. Filipovský
Georges & Jehan	Voskovec & Werich
Villon	B. Záhorský
Kateřina	J. Švabíková
Zebračka	Molnárová
Vykladačka	B. Waleská
Nuzák	J. Savrda
Královský prévôt	F. Černý

I. Finale: Hej, pane králi:… Všici

PŘESTÁVKA

Obraz 9.

Tanec Lotte Goslarová

Obraz 10. Je s tím hlídání

Purkmistr	J. Plachta
Prévôt	F. Černý

Obraz 11. Svět na ruby

Voskovec & Werich

Obraz 12. Choré srdce

Zebračka	Molnárová
Villon	B. Záhorský
Georges & Jehan	Voskovec & Werich

Tanec Lotte Goslarová

Obraz 13. Večeře pro dva

Kateřina	J. Švabíková
Purkmistr	J. Plachta
Filip	F. Filipovský
Villon	B. Záhorský
Georges & Jehan	Voskovec & Werich
Prévôt	F. Černý

Obraz 14. Františku, už tě nepočítají…

Villon	B. Záhorský
Prévôt	F. Černý
Kateřina	J. Švabíková
Kat	

* * *

Tanec Lotte Goslarová

Obraz 15. Pěvecký festival

Voskovec & Werich

Obraz 16. Vražda

Villon	B. Záhorský
Vykladačka	B. Waleská
Zebračka	Molnárová
Filip	F. Filipovský
Hlídač	J. Savrda

Epilog Všici

Děje se v Paříži kolem r. 1455

Protože Lotte Goslarová mění své tance, uvádíme jejich dnešní pořad na červené příloze.

Balada z Hadrů: a program from The Liberated Theater

a highly artistic people, and my friendship with the new painters like Kokoschka and many of the young composers has remained an unforgettable enrichment in my life. It would have been impossible during the constant travels with the Peppermill. But it was too good to last forever.

Lotte Goslar in the dressing room of The Liberated Theater in Prague, dressed for *Fille de Joie*. Photo: Press Photo Service

The Dancing Clown

by Voskovec and Werich, The Liberated Theater, Prague

It is difficult to write about the art of Lotte Goslar for those readers who have never seen her, but it is far more difficult to write for those who have. It is characteristic of a fine picture to make description a difficult task as it is equally difficult to inject good literature into an illustration. The same must be said for the dance of Lotte Goslar.

She expresses conceptions and ideas of the dance in such a true dance form that it is practically impossible to translate them into another form of expression.

We never heard of a dance artist who dared to choose such abstract and improbable subjects as Goslar.

After all it doesn't mean anything to entitle a dance *The Disgruntled*. We are used to worse things, such as the terminology of the different rhythmic dance groups. But to achieve such an effect with this dance – which really does not step out of bounds of its title – that the audience roars with laughter and breaks into spontaneous applause at certain movements, surely, for this, a remarkably comical imagination is necessary.

Another dance is called: "The Artist in Person." On the stage Lotte Goslar appears in a costume which represents a cross between Mephisto, Faust and Dante from the Wax Figure Museum, all this motheaten and slightly forbidding. The nose reaches beyond the chin, a feather on the hat and the eyebrows constantly raised in admiration of his own ingenuity. Without expressing anything concrete, the dancer behaves so indescribably in this costume that the onlooker gets the right idea about the immeasurable ridiculousness in the vanity and the so-called creature mystery of the artist.

Lotte Goslar's way of working, by the way, explains the unusual effectiveness of her art. In her rehearsals, she improvises on certain themes which she cannot define at the beginning, and then in a purely emotional way she gradually conceives the expression of a "something" which perhaps nobody has yet looked for in the dance.

When we saw Lotte Goslar for the first time, we longed very much to have her in our theater. Today this wish has become a reality. We are glad that our audience appreciates her as much as we did.

The Fortune Teller

Shortly before Erika Mann asked me to join the Peppermill for its engagement in the U. S. A. – actually during my time with the Liberated Theater in 1935 – friends of mine asked me to come with them to the countryside outside Prague to visit an amazing woman: a middle-aged peasant who could neither read nor write and who lived with her children in great poverty in a hut outside the city. There was also a pig and a goat. And maybe a husband. My friends had been told that she was a fortune teller of amazing power. None of us took that seriously, but just for a lark one afternoon we travelled to her little village. She was not in, but one of her children was, a hungry-looking little girl, about six years old, who told us in Czech (which my friends spoke and translated to me), that her mother was in the field to dig potatoes. She did not know when she would be back. Then the girl vanished into a dark corner, where she remained during our entire visit. The whole house was really nothing more than one room which obviously served as kitchen, bedroom and living space for the entire family. It also was in unbelievable disorder. Everywhere there were pots and pillows, broken toys and firewood and tools and dirty dishes. After a long time the woman arrived from the field with a sack of potatoes slung over her shoulders, obviously annoyed to find strangers in her house. My friends translated some of the heated conversation. She was not in the mood, she said at first. Eventually she gave in and, after asking for the money in advance and telling us to be silent, it all began. She was a short sturdy woman with a wrinkled, tired, really old face and big dirty hands. The first thing she did was to get herself into a trance. She crouched down on the floor, her head bent and her hands tightly clasped. After a while she started trembling and grinding her teeth. She threw her head back, her eyes rolled, and out of her strangely distorted lips came the weirdest gurgling and pecking sounds. This lasted perhaps three or four minutes, when suddenly she totally relaxed in a manner that I can only call miraculous. Her old worn-out peasant's wrinkled face became that of a young and even beautiful country girl, like what you may see at a folk dance or at a fair. Her cheeks were slightly blushing; her eyes were now almost closed. She got up from the floor, totally relaxed, and in a soft and pleasant and almost dreamy voice, she asked me to walk a few steps, then turn and walk back. Several times: back and forth, back and forth. Maybe ten times. Then she said, "Lottinka, you are a dancer. But you dance in an unusual way. You will go to America. There you will have big success. But be careful. You are too modest. That is not good. I will help you. I shall look over your left shoulder and warn you. I will always be there."

This was a long, long time ago, and I don't remember how it all ended. Did I really believe that this strange lady – or anyone else – could tell my future? She could not possibly have heard of me. We came to her home unannounced. Nobody had given her my name or any other detail about my life. But I did go to America (although at that time I did not even know about it). And I do use dance in a special way. But I don't think I'm all that modest, although throughout all these many years, I've occasionally thought of her looking over my shoulder egging me on. Do I believe in that magic power? Not really. But then also not really not. What I know for sure, though, is that there is so much I don't know.

Off to America

At the end of my engagement at the Liberated Theater in Prague, I received a letter from Erika Mann asking me to rejoin the Peppermill for a season in New York and a tour throughout the United States. But first the whole company was to assemble at Max Reinhardt's castle "Leopoldskron" in Salzburg. He had invited about 15 of the most famous and influential American show business stars and tycoons for an informal evening, during which we would play samples of our programs in order to give our future plans a boost. Marlene Dietrich was there and so was Helen Hayes with her husband. There was no stage and no adequate lighting. The whole thing took place by candlelight in an enormous grotto-like hall, stuffed with antique furniture and with a floor of huge flagstones. I don't think anybody really liked what we did and we ourselves hated it. It was the typical grand promotional affair that so often backfires. Nevertheless, it helped to solidify the American engagement. Erika and Klaus soon left for New York City, and I, after a few solo concerts in Brussels and Switzerland with my own pianist, and a trip to Paris to see Hans Sahl, flew to Rotterdam to join Therese Giehse and Magnus Henning, our pianist/composer, for our journey to the New World. On arrival I learned that in the meantime Erika had sent a telegram telling us that things had not yet been quite settled in New York and that it was necessary to postpone our trip. She would let us know when to start. So we waited. And waited. Until finally her next telegram told us to come immediately without any delay. Unfortunately, it was now October, the time of the big and dangerous storms, and there was only one ship available that we could book: a freighter that, once upon a time, had been an island-hopping, colonial cruiser. Like all freighters it was allowed to carry up to 20 passengers in addition to its cargo and crew. Which of course meant that we had to forego the anticipated luxury of the big ocean liner that had already been paid for and to accept instead the inferior accommodations of an ancient freighter. So we three, quite upset, went to the dock, and that is where several ominous things happened that should have forewarned me. First I was handed a book that a witty friend of mine had sent to me as a bon voyage present with the title "Famous Sea Disasters." I am not really superstitious, but still... The next thing: We saw our ship! The brochure had shown the picture of a gleaming white vessel with two impressive large funnels, but what we saw there lying before us was a rusty minor river boat. And it had only one funnel. One look at it and I was already seasick although I was still standing on solid ground. When I asked about the missing chimney, the answer was a calm, "Oh, that broke off several years ago." Believe me, it sounds even more discouraging in Dutch. I speak the language fairly well because I have toured many times all over Holland. I discovered that if you know German and English, and mix them in the right proportions you have it made. Before we could board the ship, we had to go into a shed for a medical examination. Actually it was only an eye test. The doctor was a very short and very intense old man with bushy black eyebrows and a large blond wig that forever slipped from side to side depending on which way he tilted his head. He was standing on a wooden crate which brought him eye to eye with his victims, all the time brandishing a rather large flashlight much like a sword in the hands of a midget Samurai. Giehse was first. Then came Henning and then I. But no sooner was he finished with me and I was on my way out, than he called me back and gripping my head as in a vice, he started rummaging through my hair to find out if maybe I was trying to smuggle lice into the U.S.A. The reason obviously was my forever unruly hair. Needless to say, Giehse was in stitches. In spite of my being found innocent, we still were not allowed to go on board because they had not finished loading the cargo of huge cement blocks into the belly of our little freighter. I was scared stiff since not only had the ship sunk down to the point where the waves were lapping over the deck, but I also overheard the men argue loudly about the danger of adding even one more of the huge blocks. But that was not the worst. When finally we were able to board, the real nightmare started. However let me tell you first about a strange thing: I started to feel sorry for our ship, that little nutshell that was willing, against all odds, to brave the big wild ocean and deliver us to America. As if she was a living creature who, no matter how abused she was, had not lost her spirit. I could not help but feel a certain kinship to her. Poor little darling I thought. *Arme kleene schatje.*

So now we went on board and soon found out what we had gotten ourselves into. The year was 1936 and all worthy ocean liners were already equipped with stabilizers, a device that makes seasickness obsolete. But our little freighter wasn't granted any such luxury. Once we were out in the open sea, she really rolled, being thrown from side to side and at the same time from bow to stern. Up to the crest of watery skyscrapers and in the next split second without any warning down, down, down into the deepest valleys. She was supposed to arrive in New York after seven days. But she needed fourteen. Twice she was driven back toward Rotterdam and several times she couldn't move in either direction, Holland or America. Only up and down and from right to left or vice versa. She heaved and howled and trembled, but she couldn't make it.

On the first day of our voyage we were introduced to the other people on board. First we met the captain, a big, sturdy and bony man with a baby-pink round face and the typical seaman's sideburns and chin whiskers, who had chosen, as we later discovered, to stay – and sleep – in his small upstairs look-out room for the entire trip. To meet him we had to climb a rather dangerous winding staircase whose tight circular design naturally compounded our by now already raging nausea. Giehse and Henning were still somehow upright, but I remember that I had to negotiate the ascent on all fours. Once up in the captain's overheated nest-like attic, we were greeted with a friendly but much too loud "Daag." He insisted that we join him in a toast to the journey with an "Oude Klare," the very potent Dutch equivalent of gin or vodka, which he poured from a good sized bottle that was part of a large collection visible under his bed. Then his jovial mood suddenly changed and he said: *"Dat's jammer dat wej allemaal moeten verdrinken"* (Too bad that we all will have to drown). But why? We soon found out. Among the passengers there was a group of eight student *"pastorjes,"* priest-missionaries on their way to do good somewhere in an unkempt part of the world, and it seemed that our superstitious nautical shepherd believed – according to sea lore – that having *"pastorjes"* on a ship was bound to lead to doom since the devil would try everything to destroy them. His mood changed again rather quickly with one more *"Oude Klare."* From under the bed he fished a phonograph and a record by Richard Tauber. He assured us that he could sing louder than the famous tenor. Since he had turned the volume to molto pianissimo and he himself was screaming at the top of his lungs, he of course proved himself to be right. To the roar of *"Dein ist mein ganzes Herz"* we left, Giehse and Henning staggering down the corkscrew staircase and I falling after them. I don't think our captain ever noticed that we were gone.

Once down on the deck we saw the eight *"pastorjes,"* all of them hanging over the railing with green/gray faces, like so much wash on a clothesline; It was not the best possible time to introduce ourselves. We never saw them again. And it still bothers me that one day I found one of their sandals on the deck. Without a *"pastorje"* in it. There were nine more passengers on board, but I was much too sick to mingle. Giehse, much sturdier than I, later told me some horrendous stories. She had figured them all out. According to her, there was one gangster from Chicago, who had boarded the ship with several huge crates labeled

"Salted Peanuts" but actually containing smuggled machetes; an overripe Australian nymphomaniac in constant pursuit of the *"pastorjes"*; and a Belgian widow, who did not speak one word of her native French.

And then, of course, there was the crew. I'm sure there must have been more of them, but during the entire voyage until the very last day, I saw only six, who, we were told, were hired as combination stokers-cooks-waiters-maids-and-deck hands. We were convinced that they came from some institutional labor pool. Giehse suggested a minimum security prison, but Henning was more for an insane asylum. Obviously they were very poor, and we probably would have felt sorry for them if we ourselves had not been so much in need of some comfort. Their uniforms and aprons were unbelievably dirty and so were their thumbs that were forever planted in our soups. And among them, I swear, they didn't have more than nine teeth, which all looked like the moss-covered pilings we had seen in the harbor. Our cabins were in the front of the ship, but the dining room was in the back, and for every meal we had to walk over a long stretch of deck that had on one side the aforementioned railing but on the other side only a thick rope to hold onto for dear life. In the tug-of-war between the howling storms and ourselves clinging to the rope, it was an absolute miracle that we were not swept into the sea. Why then did I not just stay in my cabin? Maybe the following will explain that. Since in her youth our ship had been a quasi-luxury cruiser, she still showed some remnants of her past elegance. Everything in these cabins – the beds, the sofas, the walls, and even the floors and ceilings – was covered with what once must have been thick red plush. It also was soaking wet and obviously had been so for decades. The resulting, truly memorable, smell, mixed with that of rancid oil, was what drove me to the deck – to get a breath of fresh air, even though it could be the last one I might ever breathe. On top of this, someone had tried to conquer the evil smells with a very potent cleaning fluid, with no effect whatsoever. Except that it acted as an aphrodisiac on our crew. I once met one of them in the dark hallway between the cabins. In one hand he was carrying a tray and in passing he plunged the other one on my bosom, saying with a grin: "Was dat mooie?" Which simply means: "Was that good?"

The smells, the soups, and the unending *mal-de-mer* finally brought me to a monumental decision: I would take a bath. First I went to see Giehse, who I knew had taken one, to ask about the risk involved. In her reassuring Bavarian accent she said, "It's okay – as long as you wash yourself afterwards." There was one obstacle though – the door to the bath-room didn't want to open. It was a very heavy and very large door. Also the ship was rocking and rolling like mad. I pushed and pushed, but nothing happened. Until suddenly, with a tremendous howl, the door flew open, carrying me with it, and with another even louder crash – after first throwing me into the chamber – finished the job by shutting itself closed for eternity and leaving me inside with the knowledge that I would never, ever be able to get out again. But after a few moments of simply being stunned, I regained my composure (and stubborness) and opened the faucets. A brownish-yellow flood rushed out of both pipes – each one boiling hot, although one was marked "cold" – which made the tub resemble a giant cup of tea, especially since the bottom soon was covered with rusty metal splinters that looked not unlike tea leaves. However, in no time, because of the constantly changing tilt of the ship, the entire steaming brew splashed over the edge of the tub, barely missing me. And then some of the water threw itself into the ocean by way of two broken portholes that a moment later were used by a huge ice-cold wave to tumble in and crash into the bathtub, where it mixed itself with the still running hot tea, and, taking me along, spread out over the entire tile floor. There followed an ominous calm, and reasoning that the water on the floor couldn't possibly be dirtier than that in the tub had been – and that at least it was lukewarm – I sat down on the tiles looking for the large ballshaped piece of soap that I had glimpsed dancing in and out of the broken portholes. Only to hear a strange gurgling sound and to see that the water was disappearing between the tiles. Where to? I had no idea. It just vanished. And I fled. To my amazement I found that it was much easier to get out of the bathroom than it had been to get in. Of course I was not an iota cleaner than before. On the contrary.

When we arrived three days later in Hoboken, we were in a truly miserable mood, blaming Erika not only for our own troubles, but for all the ills in the entire world. On the pier were Klaus and Erika waving happily at what they believed were their friends. But on the bow of the ship stood three grim statues – Giehse, Henning and I – bent on retribution and vengeance, shaking their dirty clenched fists. A fine reunion!

And what should happen? Instead of being cleared right away for our entry into the U.S.A., we were sent to Ellis Island. The reason? Our sponsor, the publisher Alfred Knopf, was supposed to have been at the pier when we landed. But since nobody quite knew when we would arrive (and when we finally did, it was on a long holiday weekend), Mr. Knopf was at his country estate, somewhere in Connecticut I believe. But all's well that ends well. No sooner had we been booked into Ellis Island and given blankets for sleeping on some cots than word came that we had been cleared after all. Of course it took quite a few hours more before we got to our comfortable hotel in Manhattan. But once there, I took the longest, most luxurious, and sweetest-smelling bath I've ever taken in my entire life.

A Propos Aging

Once a little boy asked me: "How old are you?" I said, "You guess." "Fifteen?" he said. I can't tell you how flattered I was. Actually I was way into my fifties. "No, dear," said I, "I'm a little older. Guess again." "A hundred?" he said.

Whatever age you tell people, they will always add at least ten years. So, why ask? And why answer?

When I turned fifty, all I could think of was – when did that happen? I really hadn't noticed. For me the best part of life started about that time.

When people ask me how old I am, I feel like being put on display in the sideshow of a circus. "Ladies and gentlemen! Here is the man with the 100 tattoos! And over there you see the bearded lady! And on this side we present the aging dancer!"

We had a wonderful doctor in New York who took care of all the problems a dancer could have. When I developed some excruciating pain in one knee, I went to him for help and told him that for a new dance I had to go way down in a deep plié. "No," he said, "you don't have to. Just do what you *can* do *well*." And that really is the secret.

One thing I like about my cats: they never ask how old I am. Neither have they ever told me, "Listen, you look awful today! Put some make-up on. And comb your hair!" What a relief!

On second thought – maybe they did tell me, but I didn't listen.

While I was visiting a friend in his casting office in Hollywood, a little boy came in. "Mister," he said, "I need a job. I'm six years old and I haven't achieved a thing."

Not wanted: any teenager coming backstage to tell you, "My grandmother saw you when she was a little girl."

Even worse: a friend you haven't seen since kindergarten exclaiming, "Lotte! You haven't changed one bit!"

So Much Luck (II)

The Peppermill, Erika Mann's fabulous anti-fascist literary Kabarett that had been such a sensation in Europe, was a total flop in America when it opened in January 1937 in New York. There were many reasons. The actors, including the great Therese Giehse, did not speak English fluently, and the themes of many songs and sketches were not really interesting to New York audiences. Also, America was still quite "isolationist." Aside from that, this form of political Kabarett was totally unknown in the USA. The engagement, planned by the Columbia Concert Corporation for a New York season at the Chanin Theater and a subsequent coast-to-coast tour throughout the States, was cut down to one week.

I shall never forget the first rehearsal that was attended by the manager, who had booked us but had never seen us before. He couldn't believe what he heard and saw. Shaking his head in desperation, he kept on saying, "I don't understand it. I don't understand it!" Whereupon the actors, thinking that he simply meant he couldn't hear them acoustically, started shouting and finally screaming louder and louder, until the man got up and left. Of course none of that helped to create a friendly atmosphere before the première, and it did not come as a surprise when, one week after our opening, our own management had the piano removed, so that even with the best will and intent, we couldn't do the show.

I myself had a separate encounter with the manager. After he saw me do *The Disgruntled* at rehearsal, he came backstage and smiling broadly (smiling broadly, mind you!) he kept on repeating over and over, "It's ugly, Lotte, ugly, ugly, ugly." Not knowing much English, I had no idea what "ugly" meant, but seeing his smile, I mistook it for some sort of praise. So I kept on saying, "Thank you, thank you, thank you," in unison with his "ugly." I just wish I had a tape of our lovely duet.

The language problem can be a very real dilemma when you are an emigrant. After I had left Germany for good, I had to get used to speaking French, because in most countries, like Czechoslovakia and even Holland, people did not want to speak German any longer even though it had been their second language. Of course that was only a minor problem compared with everything else, and eventually I spoke

French quite fluently. But then I had to switch to English when I came to New York, and that caused some new problems. My European manager Ernst Krauss had sent an introductory letter to his colleague, the American impresario Sol Hurok, and had asked me to follow this up by calling Mr. Hurok upon arrival to make an appointment. I did call, but I said to the secretary, "How can I get rid of Mr. Hurok?" "How can I get hold of him?" would have been so much better.

After the demise of the Peppermill at the Chanin Theater, through the interest and help of Alvin Johnson, the director of the New School for Social Research, we played an extra two weeks in his theater in New York to a mostly European audience. It was a success, but it came too late. The Peppermill was breaking up. I was planning to go back to Prague, when, one week before my departure, I got a call from Columbia University. Dr. Russell Potter, the Director of the Institute of Arts and Sciences, wanted to know whether I would be interested in giving a concert at McMillin Theater, for which he was just booking four evenings, entitled "4 Star Series." He had already signed Martha Graham, Trudi Schoop and Agna Enters. If I was interested, would I please meet him in the cocktail lounge at Town Hall. I almost said no. For a European ear that sounded strange. Negotiating a contract in a cocktail lounge? Well, thank God, I said yes; I signed my first American contract on a paper napkin with the picture of a rooster on it, and I am still stunned by the luck it has brought me.

The main reason for the Peppermill disaster had been the language difficulties. But that was no problem for me since I did not speak on stage. Also, everyone connected with the theater world – every producer, every director, every manager, writer and composer – had seen our show and I had been accepted. For the next ten years every engagement I got in America came directly out of our resounding flop. How unbelievably lucky I have been. After all I was totally unknown in America, with the Peppermill disaster still looming large over my future. But this, as I learned soon, was America, where everything was possible. Also, as my luck would have it, this was only the beginning. I had soon become friends – close friends – of the entire Potter family, and it was Russell who made my next two engagements possible. A colleague of his, the lecture manager Colston Leigh, had called him with a problem. He had booked the daughter of Nijinsky for a concert tour, but she had become pregnant. He needed a replacement immediately. It had to be a female dancer – from Europe – who did some special kind of dancing. I certainly fit that mold. I signed a contract for three years of solo concerts all over the USA and was now able to stay in America.

THE INSTITUTE OF ARTS AND SCIENCES
Columbia University
presents a
4-STAR DANCE SERIES

Wednesday, January 11, at 8:30

 TRUDI SCHOOP
... and her Dancing Comedians

Wednesday, January 25, at 8:30

 MARTHA GRAHAM
... and her Concert Group

Wednesday, February 8, at 8:30

 LOTTE GOSLAR
... "Europe's greatest dancing-mime"

Wednesday, March 8, at 8:30

 ANGNA ENTERS
... "America's greatest dance-mime"

 ALL RECITALS ARE GIVEN IN McMILLIN ACADEMIC THEATER
Broadway at 116th Street, New York City
All seats are reserved.
The number of subscriptions available is definitely limited.
Prices: $5.00, $4.00, $3.00, for entire series of four

Program for the Columbia University 4-Star Dance Series

Soon afterwards, the director of the Rainbow Room, the prominent New York nightclub, trying to bring concert quality into his programs, asked Russell for the name of a dancer who would qualify. There was an audition – on a sunny afternoon, way up on the 65th floor of Rockefeller Center, with the waiters noisily setting the tables for dinner and the director reclining on a large lounge chair. Was he a little tipsy? Were his eyes closed? Was he watching me at all? After I had finished my three dances, he said to my agent, "You know, she's better than Josephine Baker!" When you realize that one of the numbers I had done was "The Disgruntled" and the other two were also on the clownish side, you know how ludicrous that statement was. But it gave my agent the license to ask for a very high fee. Nevertheless, I hated every moment of this posh engagement. On the other hand, I now could stay long enough in America eventually to become a citizen.

Between 1938 and 1942 my life was nomadic and very colorful. Since I had been seen by so many different members of the theater community, the engagements I was offered were extremely varied and so numerous that I could not accept them all (for instance I had to forego joining the *Show of Shows* because of an upcoming concert tour). But I did dance, and choreograph, in Leonard Sillman's *Who's Who* and in two Vienna/Broadway Shows, *From Vienna* and *Reunion in New York*. Together with Erika Mann I went to San Francisco and Los Angeles to dance in some huge extravaganzas for charities, and in between I did a concert tour throughout Holland under the same management that had booked me into many German municipal theaters in 1933 – and then had to cancel it all when I decided to emigrate. Now the manager himself was a refugee.

Erwin Piscator asked me to create a "Mummers Dance" for his "King Lear" production with Sam Jaffee at the New School. There were also several exciting joint performances at the 92nd Street YMHA, for which no one was paid. Sponsored by TAC (Theater Arts Committee), and assembled by Edna Ocko, the editor of TAC Magazine, they were mixed programs with changing casts that involved Agnes de Mille, Jack Cole, Paul Draper, Doris Humphrey, Charles Weidman, Martha Graham, myself and many more. Of course there were also the yearly coast-to-coast concert tours for Colston Leigh and a lot of single evenings in and around New York, including one I cannot forget, because of an odd situation. Alvin Johnson had engaged me for a performance at the New School. In those days it was the custom (or maybe the law?) to play an orchestrated rendition of the national anthem over the loudspeaker before a show could begin. My pianist, waiting for our opening number, was already sitting at the grand piano on the side of the stage – in the half dark but in full view of the audience – from where a special flood light, placed on the floor, was illuminating the American flag. I have no idea how it happened, but this light was throwing a huge shadow of my pianist on the wall behind. He was not aware of it, but, tired as he must have been, all through the anthem he yawned and kept on yawning, with his giant silhouette enlarging and distorting each and every one of these unfortunate displays. I saw it all from backstage and died. But of course there was nothing I could do about it.

During all these years, many of my European friends arrived in New York. Hans Sahl came and so did Voskovec and Werich. When I had left their Liberated Theater in Prague to join Erika Mann in America, we had made plans in case they were endangered by a fascist occupation. They would send me a bogus telegram that meant that they had to leave their country, and I would try to secure them some engagement, which at that time was the only way to get exit permits. Any job would do as long as they could get out. At that time I was under exclusive contract to William Morris, Jr., and when the telegram arrived, I went to him. Through his immediate action the two – together with their composer Jaroslav Jezek – could come to the USA. The telegram he sent them was so full of professional detail, that they thought it was for real and that not only had they escaped Hitler, but had stepped into a new career in America. Actually, they had a very hard time adjusting to the New World. As with Hans Sahl, the language was the great handicap. But also, like Hans Sahl, they were able to bounce back.

Those years were a very exciting time for dancers, and I soon found myself in the middle of it all. Everyone seemed to be creating something new. There was a lot of helping one another. I lived in the "Village" (Greenwich Village), not far from my good friend Agnes de Mille, and I remember many times when a group of us would go over to her place to help with sewing her costumes. Usually she gave solo recitals, but one day she invited me to see a larger group piece she had choreographed, called *Hell on Wheels*. Among the performers was a young man named Jerome Robbins, who caught my attention immediately. Since at that time I was trying to assemble a small group myself, I asked Agnes whether she needed the young man in the near future. When she told me she didn't, I called him. He said, yes, he would be interested. Only, he had just auditioned for Ballet Theater. They had not yet called him back, but if they accepted him, he would go with them and not be available. And what do you know? They accepted him! The rest, of course, is history.

On Tour: Road Signs

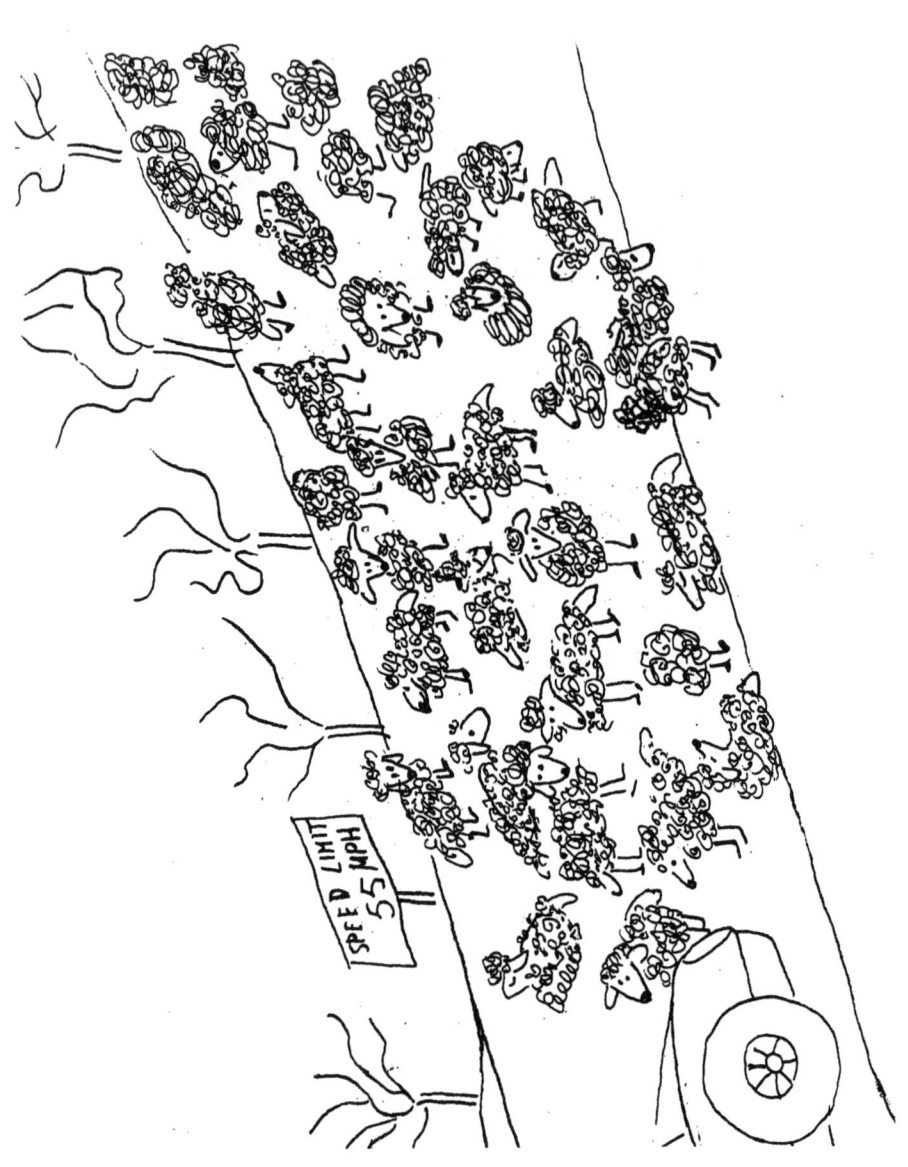

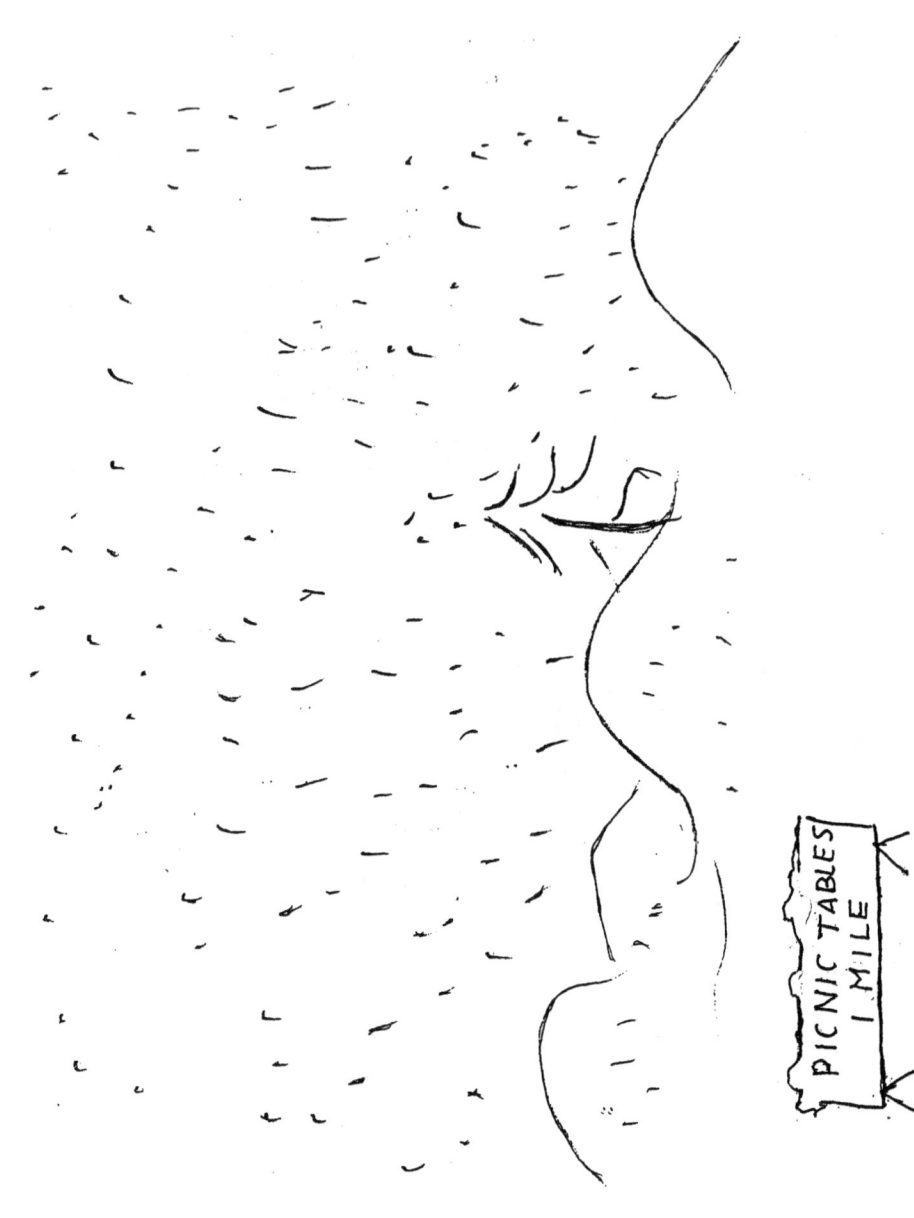

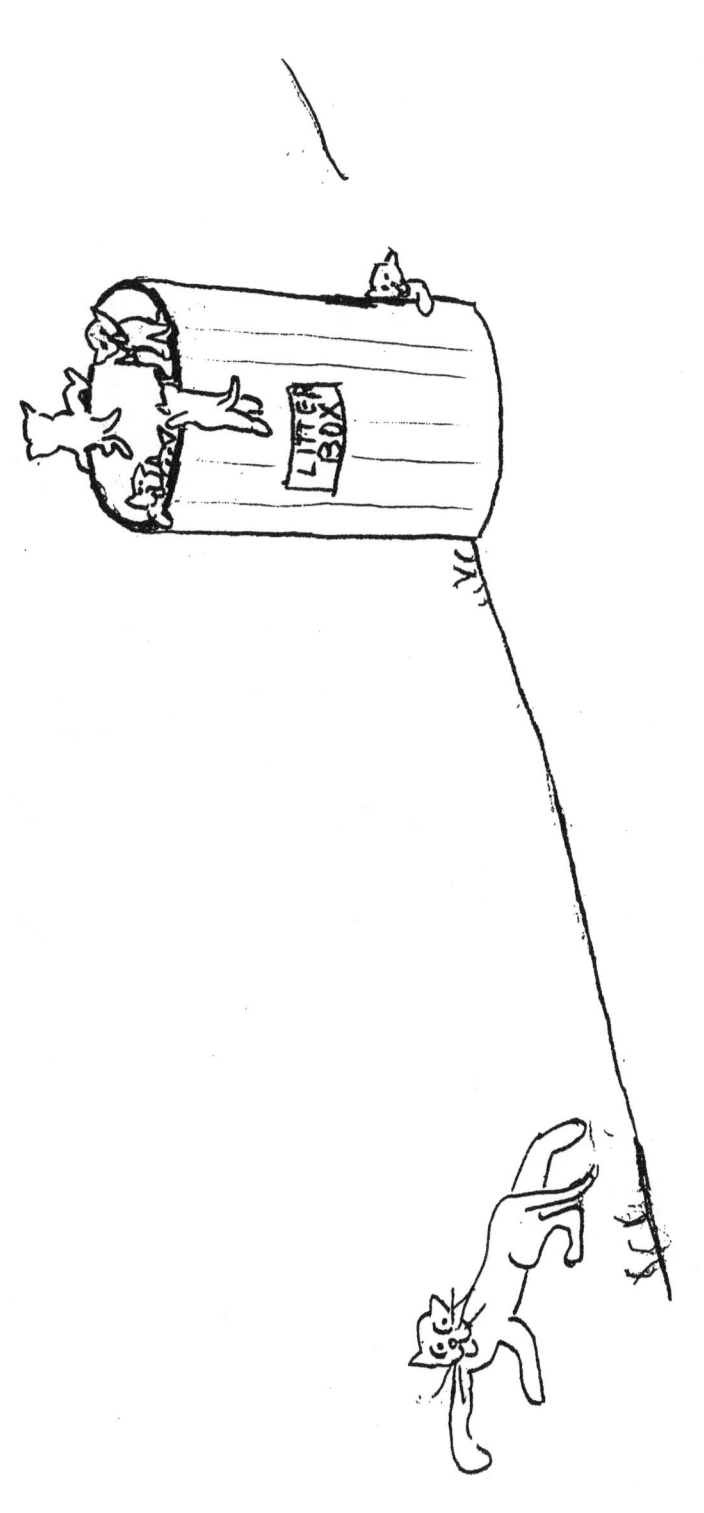

To The Rescue

The year before I joined the Turnabout Theater in 1943 was a total disaster. I had not expected that anything like that could ever happen. I had been sailing along so easily, and suddenly I was stranded. How was that possible? I had just signed with one of the best managers, Paul Schiff, the head of the former *Suddeutsche Konzertdirektion* who had emigrated to America. Two of the finest artists he represented were Artur Rubinstein and Wanda Landowska. It had seemed like a miracle when he added me to his small group of clients. But Mr. Schiff died before he could become active in my behalf, and I had to learn a lesson I was not prepared for: in America, although you don't have to give up when you are down, you can't feel secure when you are up. In spite of all the acceptance I had found in this country, I had to prove myself all over again. It seems now that my biggest mistake was not to hire a publicity manager when I had gotten so much attention in the press. I thought that would be very unethical. To blow my own horn! I suppose I was just naive about it all. After all, my profession is called show *business*. But I still feel uncomfortable about that whole matter.

So there I was without work, without income and without much hope. Of course I tried everything to survive and to create a comeback. By being very frugal with what I had earned before and by giving dance lessons, I finally ended up in a dilapidated former ballet studio on East 59th Street in New York. It was not meant to be rented as a living space, but on the sly I was able to both work and sleep there.

Several times during that year I was approached by people from the theater world who had seen me dance when I was up and functioning well. I remember one young talent scout who was convinced that I was what Broadway and Hollywood had been waiting for. He had lined up some rich entrepreneurs who were willing to spend a great deal of money on La Goslar by opening a nightclub in my name. When I told him that I wasn't exactly a sex symbol, he disagreed. Any of my clown numbers, he thought, would be a sensation if at the end I would turn it into a striptease. He also had already talked to an interior decorator who was eager to design this den of lust. The room would of course be quite dark, and the lights coming from the ceiling would look like the eyes of gorgeous oriental ladies, blinking suggestively most of the time. The chairs would be covered with plastic pillows in the shape of naked bosoms that would squeak when people sat down. What on earth had I done to inspire such nightmares?

Another attempt to rescue me came from a very different source. On one of my tours I had performed at a university in Florida. Afterwards I had met a critic for an interview; among other things he told me that he had just divorced his much adored wife for the third time. When I met him again in 1942 in New York, he had remarried the lady, a woman of extreme Garboesque beauty and deep depressions. He asked me to let her watch one of my rehearsals because he believed that my sense of humor could save her from the worst. She came and recovered instantly from her darkness, so much so that for the next days and weeks she took me on endless shopping sprees to the most expensive boutiques and loaded me with all those baubles I don't care for. She also insisted on changing my future. Actually, she knew a lot of important people from the theater, the arts and the fashion world. In my utter despair, I fell for her enthusiasm and let her go ahead. She invited twenty "important" people to my studio and asked me to dance four numbers. This event was to happen on a Sunday afternoon when there was no elevator service, so everybody, including one one-legged visitor on crutches, had to climb up three floors. Her theory was that the less comfort these guests would find, the more they would appreciate my performance. For the same reason, there were only fifteen chairs for the twenty people, so five of them had to stand or sit on the floor. Is that what is called sophistication? The invitation was for 3:00 p.m., but she arrived one full hour late, breezing in with two stunning greyhounds and looking more beautiful than ever. Afterwards there was a cocktail party at the Hotel Pierre where she was staying, so that I could meet my audience, but she did not show up. There was a great reward, however. Marc Chagall, who happened to be in New York on that day, had been in the audience. His understanding, his interest and his warmth made up for everything. But why did I subject myself to all this foolishness in the first place? As I said before, I was desperate. Is that a good excuse? No!

Shortly after that dilemma, Lotte Lenya, a good friend of mine and of Hans Sahl, came to the rescue. She had been performing with great success in a sophisticated nightclub in New York and she suggested to the owner that he engage me after she had finished. In spite of my misgivings, I stubbornly convinced myself that I could make it a success. The stage was even smaller than the one I had battled in my Peppermill days in Zürich, and in addition a baby grand piano occupied half of it. But I was determined to win. There was no time left before my opening to create new material. I had to use existing numbers and of course make some drastic adjustments. In my concert programs I often had done a piece called *Waltzmania* in which I portrayed a young girl who gets totally mesmerized whenever she hears music in three-quarter time. So much so, that at the end she is in a delirium, unable to stop even when the lights fade and the curtains close one by one in front of her. This dance always worked well on large stages. But how to translate it to a non-stage? Well, leave it to desperate Miss G. to find a solution. I thought I could make it possible and interesting by turning *Waltzmania* into a Sitz-Walzer (a sitting waltz), doing the whole number perched on top of the piano and letting only my face, my shoulders, my hands and feet, my eyes, and even my nose be mesmerized and twitch in three-quarter time. The beautiful romantic dress I wore got an appreciative "ahh" from a few tables, but the dance didn't. Perhaps the audience thought I was sick. There were quite a few worried faces staring at me. So *Waltzmania* was out.

One number I was sure could be done in the reduced space was *Little Heap of Misery*, a clown I had created as a loving spoof on the vulnerable soul of my friend Hans Sahl. All this clown wants to do is sleep. He carries a pillow and a blanket with him, so of course he *could* sleep. But no! He is on an endless track of homemade despair. By messing up even the simplest attempt, he succeeds in convincing himself that he cannot succeed. In a way this dance is an abstraction, a march of doom, starting from nowhere and after a slow progression of failures vanishing into nowhere. There is neither a beginning nor an end to his eternal unnecessary woe. This number always got a lot of laughter, and I was hoping for the same here.

But there was a problem. The music – the "Nightmare" by Clyde McCoy, with all its sobbing and crying sounds – had to be played by a combo of three musicians and that combo had to be placed close to the piano. Meaning on stage. Meaning further that there would be no room left for me. But I was not worried. When I rehearsed my program in the afternoon the place was empty and I could plan everything very carefully. I found that I did not need to use the stage at all if I was left enough room in front of it. The stage was at the short end of the nightclub's oblong space. On either side it had swinging doors leading into and out of the kitchen. The dressing room was beyond the kitchen, so both the waiters and the artists had to use these doors for their entrances and exits. When I rehearsed in the afternoon the tables were already set for the evening, and I saw with great relief that there was a good sized space left open for my dances between the front of the stage and the first row of tables.

What I didn't realize was that the place would look quite different in the evening. This was a popular nightclub, and it was very crowded. As I was standing there behind the swinging door ready to go on and trying to concentrate, people were still arriving. They had to be seated at quickly placed extra tables. I saw that my performing space was shrinking more and more until it finally was gone completely. How on earth could I do my number? Before I could solve my problem, I heard a short musical introduction and the voice of the MC: "We proudly present, etc., etc." The spotlight was searching for me but didn't find me and landed instead on a waiter trying to rush past me with a big bowl of spaghetti. Waiters were not allowed to serve during a performance. So the good man made a swift U-turn, nearly knocking me down in the process, all of which of course was registered by the glare of the spotlight. Now everybody had seen me, and in the ensuing silence I heard a loud voice saying, "What's that?" And then my music started. I made it to the center trying not to hurt people I had to push out of my way, several times being forced to whisper, "Beg your pardon," before they let me pass. And then I went underground. The only contact I had with the audience during the long middle part of the dance – when *Little Heap* tries to sleep on the floor – came from bumping into legs and chairs, but believe me there was much more going on in that netherworld. By the time the dance was finished I think people had forgotten about me – and only noticed me again when they saw me shuffling out through the swinging exit door into nowhere.

Lotte Goslar in *Little Heap of Misery*. Photo: John Lindquist

A New World

How I survived that wretched year could fill a whole book. Thank God, in retrospect most of it seems funny. Actually, I survived because luck had taken over again. Just when everything looked especially grim, a letter arrived from the Turnabout Theater in Hollywood. By chance, the three Yale Puppeteers – creators and owners of the Turnabout – had been in New York when the Peppermill opened and failed at the Chanin Theater in 1937 and they had asked me to join them when we closed. I would have accepted gladly, but there was an obstacle: California was enforcing a new curfew for "enemy aliens." As a former German, I was prohibited to be away from my home address after nine p.m. – exactly the time when the show started. But now in 1943 the curfew had been lifted. Would I come and join them?

It couldn't have come at a better time. I scraped all my pennies together and took a bus to Hollywood, an unforgettable five-day-and-night-ride in an overcrowded Greyhound without a stopover at a motel. I sat next to a double-sized, mostly snoring gentleman, who in his baby-like sleep obviously dreamed that he was at home in his own bed and, stretching himself, alternately threw me into the aisle or plunked his heavy legs across mine. Except for the short times when he woke up and devoured huge chunks from an endless supply of bread, salami, and cheese he had brought along. Being a friendly sort of chap, he always offered me what he hadn't been able to finish himself, and since I kept on declining, he simply placed some of it, minus the wrapping, in my lap.

Of course there were many rest stops at wayside restaurants when everybody left the bus for a hamburger and a Coke and French fries. Except for my friendly neighbor, who, I believe, only went into the bushes. Invariably on my return I would find him stretched out over both our seats, snoring and belching softly and smiling like an angel about whatever the salami made him dream. I didn't have the heart to wake him up, and I really don't remember how I solved the situation. Maybe I just sat down in the aisle. I only know for sure that at the end of the fifth day, we arrived in Hollywood, that my friend, with tears in his eyes, handed me the last piece of his beloved salami, and that I, totally without sleep, had to ask the driver to lift me out of the bus. All around the station there were these strange palm trees that looked like giant paint brushes, and the crescent moon was lying on her back like a boat, not upright as in Dresden. I knew I was in a new world and that I would dance again.

And dance I did. Suddenly everything seemed to fall into place. During the Turnabout years, in addition to choreography and other activities in my field, I started using the off-weekends and the short vacations to fill single concert dates in California, even venturing as far as Philadelphia and Washington, D.C. But I did not want to give solo recitals any longer. I found them poor and not good theater. And too much of Miss Goslar. To say what I wanted to say with my dances, I felt I needed the addition of other strong personalities who would provide contrast and color.

There were also technical reasons. Each of my solos needed a different costume and at that time also different make-up and often different wigs. To make these changes possible, there had to be pauses throughout the program. Twenty numbers in two sections meant eighteen pauses. What to do to make the show run smoothly? I always had fine pianists with me. So I asked them to play a short piece, like a Scarlatti or a Debussy, every time I was running back and forth to my dressing room. Sometimes that room was in the basement or on an upper floor. I cannot remember how many times I lost a shoe or a nose or slid down a staircase, hearing my pianists repeat the beginning of my next number over and over until I could give them a sign that I had survived. Those were the good old times. I still cringe when I think of the oodles of noses I've dropped on the stages of America and of the poor design of those concerts which nevertheless were considered to be successful. What it all needed, I realized, was simplicity.

During those years there was a strange division between the East and West Coast dance world. For us in Hollywood it was almost impossible to get a concert date or a management in New York. Carmalita Maracci (the fabulous Carmalita), Eugene Loring, and I even started a mini-organization to protest that situation, but without success. However, when I wrote a letter to Ted Shawn telling him that I would like to bring my small company to the "Pillow," I received an emphatic "Yes, please do come" answer, that was followed by "Papa" Shawn becoming our great supporter for many years and inviting us eleven times to dance at his beautiful Festival. I very much remember our premiere in 1954. After we had finished our show, Papa Shawn came backstage and in mock admiration went down on his knees, took my hand and said, "Will you marry me?" When I replied, "But I'm already married," he simply said, "Never mind." We became very good friends. What a kind and generous friend he was!

From left: Ted Shawn, Lotte Goslar and Thomas Leabhart at Jacob's Pillow

The Turnabout Theater

I joined the Turnabout Theater initially for three months, but I stayed for almost ten years. The theater was unique. There were two stages, one at each end of the small room. The chairs were streetcar seats that could be turned at intermission so that the audience first faced the tiny puppet stage and later the larger but still small revue stage. The puppet show was always a full-length, sophisticated play, and the revue was a mixture of songs and sketches all of it written by Forman Brown. We were six in the cast. Forman was the MC, and in addition to singing some of his own chansons, he accompanied the entire show. Elsa Lanchester, Charles Laughton's wife, was the guest star. She and I each did three numbers of our own choice. Harry Burnett, the main puppeteer, Dorothy Neuman (who also directed the show) and two more young actors, plus an occasional guest, played the rest of the four alternating programs. Everything in the show, and even during intermission, was thought out with great finesse and imagination. Charming and clever and even cozy, I think, would describe the Turnabout Theater. A far cry from the fighting spirit of the Peppermill and the Liberated Theater in Prague!

    I probably would not have stayed as long as I did had I not met my husband almost immediately after I came to Hollywood. For the first time since my childhood I would have a home again. A haven. I hadn't even realized how lost my ship had been. Bill Seehaus had been a young lawyer and judge – the only one in the small town of Gardelegen in Germany. Not being Jewish, he had been able successfully to defend people of all races even after 1933. But in 1937 he was arrested and led through the whole town with a sign around his neck saying, "Slave of Jews." Soon after that, in 1938, he was able to emigrate, of course having to leave everything he owned in the name of the state. With 100 marks in his pocket and a gold ring with one small diamond on his finger (which he bought in order to sell if needed) he left for England and later America to begin a long time of insecurity. The ring was never sold. It became my wedding ring.

    Before I met Bill, who at that time was a shipping clerk in a pants factory in Los Angeles, my landlady had told me about "that wonderful guy." "You've got to meet him – you'll love him." Of course that turned me off right away. Who was to tell me whom to love? But on the day we finally did meet in front of the house where I lived, I took one look at him in the half-dark, and all I could think was: "Help!" During that time Charles Laughton often came to the Turnabout and sometimes picked me up on his way. He had just arrived in his elegant Chauffeur-driven limousine. I heard (and didn't hear) the honking of the horn. Bill had also offered me a ride! So as if in a daze I said: "Thank you, Charles. I'm going with Mr. Seehaus!" And followed Bill into his third-hand 1928 Model T Ford rattletrap – and into his life.

Bill died in 1959. I was touring with my Company in Europe, and he was to join us in Vienna for Christmas. On the day of our premiere, Christmas Day, I received a call from Hollywood. A stranger's voice asked, "Is this Mrs. Seehaus?" "Yes." "Mr. Seehaus died this morning." Just like that.

Because we had been sold out for the two performances, the Austrian manager refused to cancel the shows, and we did them. I was split into two people: one totally numb doing everything like a puppet and the other observing it all and finding it unbearably shallow and cheap. And then I flew "home." For a full year I did not dance; I couldn't even hear music. What helped me back, I think, was walking through the California woods, drinking in the color of green. And of course time does heal.

Lotte and her husband Bill: the first new car

During my Turnabout years, Charles and Elsa and Bill and I had become good friends. We spent many weekends together in their beautiful home in Pacific Palisades on top of the then still totally unspoiled coast line. We loafed in the sun or hiked on the trails up into the hills and mountains of Santa Monica to see or pick wildflowers or drove to some deserted beach for a picnic and a swim. This was the time when Charles was especially vulnerable. Because he had been forced by some ironclad contracts to play one mediocre film after another and had done so in a routine manner (earning him the reputation of being a ham – which he could be when his heart was not in his work) – he was considered to be "box office poison." But single-handedly, he reversed all of that by starting his now famous readings of Shakespeare and the Bible, first trying it all out on veterans in hospitals (and on Bill and me and other friends) and then going on the lecture circuit. There was first a resounding howl from the movie colony. Charles Laughton, the superstar, was going on a lecture tour! Poor Charles! To sink so low. But it became a triumph for him. In no time other film stars tried to copy him, albeit with less success. And as in his successful past, he was once again besieged with film offers and did some of his finest work. I always admired Charles for that. For his belief – I share so fervently – that you have to love what you do, to succeed.

Charles was totally one-track-minded about whatever he was interested in, be it Shakespeare, the Bible or a collection of limericks, and Bill and I were willing guinea pigs. It was fascinating to hear him read these ancient texts as if they were today's language. But I'm sure it wasn't always easy for Elsa. I remember in particular one lunch. The cook had just balanced a tower-high soufflé into the dining room and Elsa was calling all of us to "come and get it." But in the next room Charles, Bible in hand, had buttonholed Bill: "Listen to this, Bill. Just one sentence!" and for the next half hour there was no way to unglue the two or rescue the soufflé.

So much has been said and written about the Laughtons. I remember them as our friends and as the great artists they were. In those leisurely hours in their home, they were real and true. The first time I met Charles, he was in his garden. He was sitting, in his pajamas, on a large branch in a tree, tending to his cascading fuchsias and, peeking like Puck through the leaves. He gave me a very warm welcome. That was not a put-on, it was the genuine Charles. And I have always felt that no matter what problems they might have had to overcome, there was a strong bond between them in their tastes and aspirations that made us feel good to be with them.

As outstanding as Elsa was in her film roles, I think her greatest talents showed when she sang the chansons Forman Brown had written for her. She was totally unique and a master in enriching the stories she told. With absolutely nothing, she was able to fill her characters with three-dimensional life and to let you in on the past, present and future of the person she portrayed, in addition to painting a whole world around the character. I've never encountered that kind of special talent in anyone else, except maybe in the work of Tracy Ullman, who is also English. And add to this her ribald, Rabelaisian humor and the fine-tuning of the double-entendres that she so masterfully underplayed. She is unforgettable!

Almost every night when he was not doing a film, Charles came to pick up Elsa toward the end of the show. There was always a high chair for him in front of the closed puppet stage. So each time, he saw the finale: a Good Night song by the whole Company. In my entire life I have never had stage fright when I danced. Excitement yes, but never fear. However that song was my undoing. To stand there with my colleagues, in a beautiful gown, being myself, Lotte G., not a character, but a private person, saying Good Night to the audience! It just killed me. After Charles had seen that catastrophe two or three times, he couldn't stand it any longer. He came backstage and said: "I don't understand you! I have been a guest in your house, and you have always made me feel welcome. But in that song you behave as though you want to crawl into a hole. Don't you know that the stage is your home and the people in the audience are your guests? You have invited them. Talk to them. Don't chase them away!" This was one of the best lessons I learned from anyone. And it worked like magic. From that day on I have always felt totally at ease when I spoke or even sang to audiences. Through Charles's words I discovered that I had been on an ego trip. I had been thinking: How do *I* look? Will *I* remember my lines? Can *I* make it across the stage? Will they like *me*? Instead of *giving* something, a simple greeting, to the friends I had invited. You cannot let your ego spoil it. I have often shared this wisdom of Charles with young performers, and almost always they have told me later that it worked for them also, like magic.

Lotte backstage with Charles Laughton, Elsa Lanchester, Bill Seehaus and Mrs. Cecil B. DeMille. Photo: United Photography Service

My Film Career

My film career has one definite distinction: it didn't exist. When I first came to Hollywood in 1943 to dance at the Turnabout Theater, some well-meaning friends predicted fame and fortune for me. "You'll be a big film star," they said. Only, I was not in the least interested. I was perfectly happy with what I had done all along: inventing my own dances and performing them in theaters. I just wanted to "do my own thing." I didn't see myself in movies, where I would have to adjust to somebody else's taste.

However, when I saw the wonderful animated films of the UPA group (United Productions of America), films like "Gerald McBoing-Boing" and "Mr. Magoo", I felt such a kinship that I called them and asked whether and where I could see more of their work. Their answer came as a surprise. They told me that they had come many times to the Turnabout Theater to see my dances and they suggested a meeting to discuss possible future collaborations. So now began a wonderful creative time with three of the leading artists of the group: John Hubley, Bobe Cannon and T. Hee. They all had worked with Disney, but had left to create their own distinct and very different style. Their studios were modest, just a row of small bungalows around a tiny pond, nothing spectacular or glamorous. But the spirit of inventiveness and daring avant garde was enormous.

Bobe made some preliminary tests and the first story conference was scheduled. Then it was cancelled without any explanation. And for nearly two months I did not hear from anyone, except an occasional secretary announcing another postponement – a strange development after having been treated with so much openness and unconditional friendship. I was stunned, until I learned that there was an explanation after all. This whole upheaval had happened at the height of the McCarthy era, and Hubley had been blacklisted. In order not to endanger UPA he had left the group, and of course the plan of making films with me was postponed endlessly and actually never came to life again.

After I started my Pantomime Circus in 1954, I was almost constantly on tour with my company, both in America and Europe, but I kept in touch with Bobe and sometime in the early sixties he called with good news. He had been offered a chance to make a recruiting film for the Navy, and wanted to use this opportunity to try out a new invention we both had been very much interested in. It replaced animation with live action for the "story boards," which meant that instead of just being the model for the drawings, I could dance out the entire action. The camera would register only the contours of body and face, color was to be overlaid afterwards in large free-style splashes. The result was amazing. Bobe let me design a befuddled *Fairy Godmother* and we made the film in broad daylight, in front of my garage in Hollywood, using a bedsheet as background. And, lo and behold, it won a first prize – although it was so short, that, if you blinked, you might have missed it. Nevertheless, it proved to us that the new process was workable, and it also induced an English film-maker friend of Bobe's to produce the films that UPA had planned with me before. By that time I had moved to New York, so our films were to be made there.

But before he could join us – in 1964 – Bobe died.

This ended a dream of starting something of quality, small at first, but allowed to grow. I have always believed in small beginnings and always shied away from big announcements before one could be sure of being on the right track. I love the small corners, where one can venture into unused fields without any interference – even including the pressure of success. Not that I don't like success. I do. But it has no business taking over, when you need being alone with your imagination.

I recently looked again at some of Bobe's test footage, and I found it interesting and "of today." Maybe there is still some life in it? We'll see!

Obviously, each time it was fate that interfered with the plans to work with filmmakers I admired. In New York, Hans Sahl had introduced me to one of the truly greats: Eugen Shuftan, the brilliant cameraman whose career had started in the Berlin of the twenties, when he – together with a bunch of young unknowns including Billy Wilder and Robert Siodmak – had made the avant garde film, *Menschen am Sonntag* (People on Sunday) that made them all famous overnight. He once told me that they had made it on a shoestring and that they never knew where the money for the next day's shooting would come from, unless someone's rich uncle would rescue them or one of them still owned a watch that could be sold or pawned. Quite often, after a day's work, he would hide the camera under a tree in the park where they were shooting, so that it couldn't be reclaimed by the pawnshop. Shufty – that's what we all called him – was an emigrant when we met, like all of us, but he found himself in an especially difficult situation. In spite of the distinguished films he had made in France with Marcel Carné and Jacques Prévert before he came to America – including *Quai des Brumes*

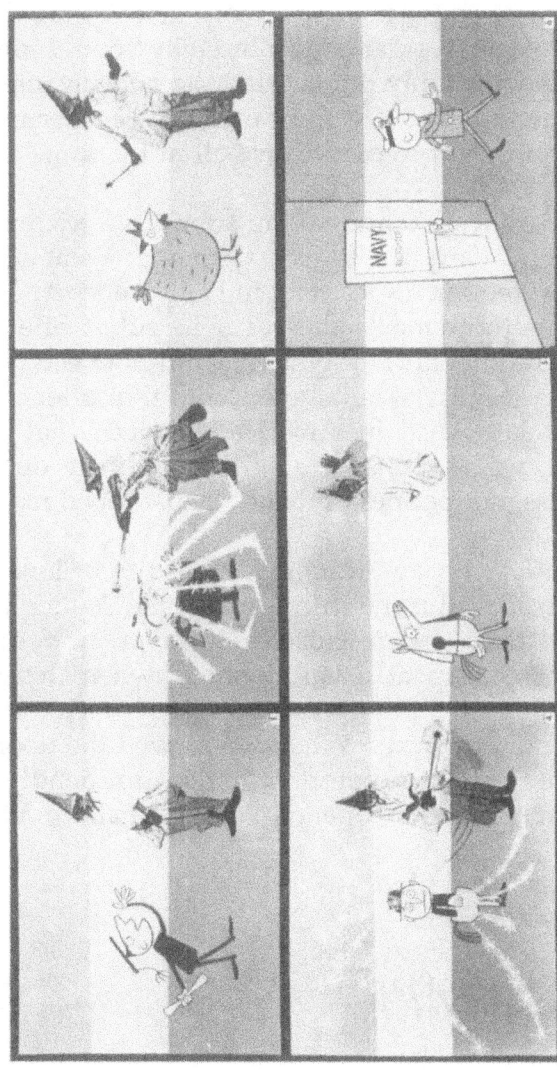

Extract from the television film animation of Lotte's *Fairy Godmother* (1957) directed by Robert "Bobe" Cannon and Chris Jenkyns

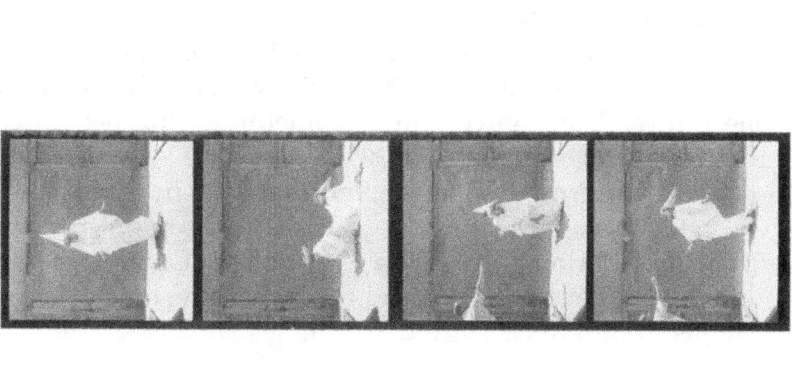

Lotte in rehearsal for *Fairy Godmother* with the director "Bobe" Cannon

(*Port of Shadows*) – he could not get a work permit here. The entire time I knew Shufty, in New York and later in Hollywood, I remember him to be idle. And desperate. Only the fact that he had invented the so-called Shuftan process, which allowed the camera to register objects in totally different sizes, from giant to diminutive all in the same frame, kept him above water.

He knew my work, and, having so much free time, he suggested that we make some fairytale films together. It went as far as Shufty shooting some test reels in a vacant lot in Hollywood. And then, just then, for the first time in those many idle years, he got an offer to shoot a film for the Canadian Film Board, for which he did not need the same permit. The end is history. Shufty was deluged with film offers, first in Canada and France, and later also in America. Between that and my heavy touring schedule, we were never able to coordinate our plans. So this time it was success, not politics or death, that stopped my illustrious film career.

Later Shufty won an Academy Award (I believe it was for *The Hustler*), but he was in Europe during that time, When he returned, the Academy Award offices were closed. However, he found out that he could pick the Oscar up at a certain hour when there would be an attendant in the building. Shufty couldn't drive. Neither could his wife, Marliese. So I picked them up. When we arrived the doors were locked, and it took quite a while before a rather unfriendly woman, who scrutinized us suspiciously, opened one. "What do you want?" she growled.

"My Oscar," said Shufty.
"What's your name?"
"Shuftan."
"How do you spell it?"
"S-H-U-F-T-A-N."
"First name?"
"Eugen."
"Your identification?"

Shufty showed her his passport. "OK," said the dragon. "Wait here."

"Here" was a small entry hall without any chairs. After quite a while she returned and gave Shufty something wrapped in old newspaper that could have been a large whiskey bottle someone tries to hide from a landlady or, from the police. Shufty took it in triumph. "Let's live it up!" he said. So we all went to a little coffee shop on the Sunset Strip and had coffee and doughnuts. His wrapped-up Oscar was sitting right next to him on the bench, and when he saw a young man at the next table staring at his "bottle," he started spinning a fantastic tale, in which a drunkard steals the "bottle," finds out to his great disappointment that it is only a dumb statue, and throws Oscar in the river. I think of the glamor and the hoopla that surrounds the Academy Awards. Then I remember this great humble and witty man, with the face of a friendly owl, who made history with the magic of his camera in many unforgettable films, being happy like a child and seeing the humor of it all! How we loved him!!! How we all loved him!

Another time I was approached by a small studio to play the part of a gremlin. The producer had seen me dance *The Woodsprite*, at the Turnabout Theater. On the strength of it, he thought I would be perfect. But before signing a contract, he sent me to a specialist to make a mask of my face. Out of hard rubber. That is when I should have stepped out of the whole thing. But I didn't. The place I went to was a bungalow, about the size of a two-car garage, behind a small house. Two men greeted me: the technician and a friend of his, who obviously had come in for a chat and remained with us all the time. I was asked to lie down on a large marble slab, and after covering my hair with a shower cap and putting two lemonade straws into my nostrils, the technician explained that now he would cover my entire face with plaster. "It'll feel funny," he said, "and it'll get hot when it dries. But don't worry. You won't suffocate. Nobody has died from this." ("Yet," said his friend.) "The main thing is, don't move your face. Don't breathe deeply. And don't scream. It'll only take about half an hour." Of course I was scared stiff. Out of my wits! During the time the plaster was drying on my burning face, the two guys were chatting with each other, reminiscing about their past. Maybe they were only kidding, trying to pull my leg, since I could not see them, but I swear this is what they said:

"Remember Dorothy Lamour?"

"You mean when you did her feet?"

"Sure. They had to be done, but with her rubber feet, she looked gorgeous."

I still can't believe that their conversation was more than a joke. Why on earth would any studio feature something that had to be camouflaged when there were so many beautiful feet tripping on the beaches of Santa Monica?

As I left his torture chamber, the plasterer – with great sincerity – apologized for any inconvenience he might have caused. "Of course it would have been easier for you if you were dead," he said, shaking my hand.

Because for almost ten years I performed in a very popular show in the film capital of America, always to sold out houses that sometimes could not even accommodate the biggest names in the industry, I was bound to be approached with film offers from time to time. My good friend Robert Siodmak asked me to play a Spanish dancer in one of his films, but I didn't believe I could do it justice. Several times I was asked to meet directors for future movies; the strangest encounter was the one with Alfred Hitchcock. A young agent brought me to the set where Hitchcock was shooting. In the taxi to the studio the young man explained to me that I would not actually meet the director, but nevertheless he would see me. There were quite a few people milling around the space outside of the set not in camera range, and of course I noticed Hitchcock immediately. He was standing half inside a prop telephone booth and was faking a conversation with an imaginary caterer, ordering supplies for a party he was pretending to give. I could hear everything because the booth was quite close and he spoke very loud. The dinner he was ordering was absolutely fantastic: a rump of a buffalo and eighty-eight lobsters were the least unlikely items. All the time he was watching me with piercing eyes as he obviously improvised his horrendous order. All of that lasted about ten minutes. Then he left. Without having talked either to me or to the agent. On the way home, the young man told me that Hitchcock thought I was too young for the part. "How do you know?" "I know," he said.

Cats I've Met

When I was a child, we almost always had a dog, always a German Shepherd, and each one was called "Wolf." I liked them all, but in my memory I cannot distinguish one from the other. Later in life, and especially in Hollywood and Connecticut, I always lived with a cat, and I remember each one distinctly. The only trouble is – I've almost never had a whole cat. Some of them were just more or less the remnants of what must have been at one time a handsome feline. That almost sounds as if I had been especially looking for some damaged goods. Not at all. I love whole cats. The ones with two eyes and two ears, with unbroken tails and at least some teeth and with voices you can hear and understand. But mine were hardly ever like that. Usually they came from a shelter or they were dumped on my front lawn. Your first mistake is to notice them at all. It becomes worse when you start talking to them, even if you are only saying: "Sorry, I can't take you." (Watch the very small tilt of the head, as if they were hard of hearing. All the time looking at you.) But the fatal moment arrives when you use a random name. Let's say: Pussycat, or Micky, and they react with: "How did you know?" After that everything works according to their scenario. A very soft purr. You stroke that delicious fur.

She – or he – is in your arms. You are hooked. And there you are, with a new cat to share your life.

Cats need a home with food and friendship. But more than anything else, they want freedom. And so do I. Make a pact with your cat right in the beginning, to respect each other's independence. It may not work, but you can try. Good luck!

The cats I lived with longest and remember most were Rosamunda Schlitz (who dumped me and became addicted to my husband's flannel pants), Lucky (whom I rescued when she was six weeks old, out of the motor of a truck in Chinatown, N.Y. and who therefore believed that she owned me for the next thirteen years), Zizi (the Burmese stud of uncertain but very advanced age, also called "Rambo" or "Pops" by his personal physician), and Mooky who lives with me now and is obviously only a leftover of the cat he must have been when he was born.

Rosamunda Schlitz

Rosamunda Schlitz, so named by my husband because of her pink mouth and her very slit eyes, was born to us in Hollywood. Her mother, a beautiful white cat, wearing a huge pink silk ribbon and smelling of all the most sinful perfumes in the world, appeared one day out of nowhere and stayed just long enough to drop a litter of five on my husband's bed and to nourish them for about a week without any display of mother love. Bill and I were convinced that she had escaped from an upper class harem and had been told to get rid of the brood someplace else, before the Sultan found out. All the time she didn't speak a meow and she soon vanished without an explanation, leaving us with the problem of finding a substitute mother. In due time we had planned to give all the kittens away, but Bill, the dog lover, had been unexpectedly bewitched by Rosamunda. So we kept her. She was quite beautiful in her black and white fur coat, and her mother had left her a stunning Italian Bal Masqué mask, that she wore all her life, even when she slept – and also a totally screwed-up psyche.

When Rosamunda was about two months old, one of her strong upper teeth started growing into her nose and had to be removed, which allowed the fang in her lower jaw to grow undisturbed to enormous proportions. This in turn made it impossible for her to fully close her mouth. Since her lips were very pink and slightly moist, it gave them the look of indulging in a dewy and only half-finished kiss, which of course drove all the Tom cats in our neighborhood wild. She became the Lolita of Pinehurst Road. You should have seen the toms, on a moonlit night, lined up in a half circle on our porch like candles, caterwauling and doing strange ritual dances – with stiff, stiff legs, all the while talking in a weird staccato language. Or the extremely handsome, young and silky poet, who came to the porch every morning to recline on the stonewall and, strumming his guitar, sang to her of eternal love. No, this vixen had something else in mind. She would keep her virginity intact, until the day when her Prince would come on his white horse and sweep her off her paws. And come he did. My heart stood still when I saw him for the first time, a tomcat of enormous size and mismatched proportions, bowlegged, with a big gash across his entire face, the ears in ribbons, one eye shut, and the other one with a hungry, indecent leer. There was something almost medieval about him. Brazenly he came in the daytime. I could see his shattered tail trembling above the high grass and hear his love call. Love call? The sound of a foghorn! He didn't have to wait long. Here she came, our sweet little Rosamunda, our virgin of the innocent dewy lips, crawling on her belly – on her belly! Crawling! – toward this brute. One swipe with his bowlegged paw across her face and she was his forever. The engagement was sealed as the newly weds vanished into the bushes.

About three days later – and that would happen twice a year – a sweet and very subdued pussycat came home-sweet home, to sleep again on Bill's flannel pants and otherwise make arrangements for the blessed event. Which was by no means blessed for my husband, whom she had chosen to be her midwife. On the day of the delivery, she became extremely agitated, running back and forth throughout the house, sometimes screaming and shouting orders at me, sometimes rolling on the floor and once in a while checking out the room with the basket that was to be the nursery. But she would not give birth until Bill came home at six o'clock. She was always excited about his car arriving, but on those days, total hell broke loose. She had been holding back all day, but now she could wait no longer. Screaming she ran to the basket, berating my husband, who was galloping after her. And now the most ridiculous ritual had to be followed. She insisted that Bill hold hands with her, meaning that he had to put his hand anywhere on her body, or else she stopped pressing and a half-born kitten would be dangling in mid-air out of her, until Bill held hands again. Now my husband was not the type who could endure anything like that lightly (we almost could not get married because he could hardly bear taking the blood test required). He was near fainting all the time, and all I could do was to hand him buckets of Cognac. He became more and more jolly and ended up singing some old student songs, as Rosamunda delivered the last naked bundle. For the next two weeks she – successfully – played the role of "Madonna of the Roselips," complete with halo. She was all Mother Love Incarnate.

Then she tried to hide her kittens until we gave them away. Once that period was over and done with, she tried to forget the whole inconvenience as quickly as possible. Until the next blast of the foghorn.

After five litters we had her fixed, and she promptly adjusted to that change by growing two large skin flaps, one on each side of her body, like two curtains, which, our veterinarian said, served to let any aggressive tom know: no entrance! When she saw her former Romeo, she couldn't even remember his name. But she kept thinking of herself as sexy for the rest of her life, and never gave up moistening her lips. As for him, I think he got the message.

Zizi

Zizi was something else. He came into my life after I had moved to Connecticut. For years my neighbors and I had seen him roaming the fields, sleeping behind the stone walls and stealing the suet from the bird feeder. We knew him as "that wild cat," and I did not want him to join us because Lucky was living with me. I even remember chasing him away once. But then the following events took place. First one winter my neighbors, great cat lovers, started feeding him. And then they moved to New York and asked me to take over. That did it. I started arguing with myself, that it might be good for Lucky to have a cat friend when I'm on tour. The neighbors who had fed her when I was away had told me that she was very lonesome. But I think all my reasonings were only excuses. The fact is that I've always liked black cats and I thought he was very handsome: a Burmese with glistening fur, broad shoulders, shining eyes and whole bouquets of whiskers. Nobody else agreed, but for me he was very beautiful. I must admit though that he had one flaw. Most of his teeth were missing, and those that were left looked like a battlefield. To see him yawn was a disaster.

Since he was not fixed (our vet thought he was too old), I hesitated for a while because of Lucky, but then one day I asked him in. Of course he had eaten the food I had put out for him, but the moment I came close, he vanished. Until someone told me that cats react favorably when they hear "zizi, zizi," which supposedly is the sound their mothers used to call them. It worked! After a week or two, he started taking food out of my hand. And after another few days, he accepted my invitation and moved in. I mean moved in lock, stock, and barrel. Like everything in his life, he did it abruptly and totally. He had decided to trust me and that was that. What this all did to Lucky is a grievous story in itself, which I don't want to touch on here. She never forgave me. For her it was a betrayal, although I went overboard trying to make her feel that she was No. 1. She wanted me to throw him OUT!!! So now Zizi owned my house. And me. Pretty soon he taught me the few sounds with which he planned to communicate. To announce his homecomings, his voice resembled one of those cheap little toy trumpets that people blow on New Years Day. Whenever I heard his toot-toot, I knew Zizi was not far away. Also, when I fed him something especially tasty, he gobbled it up in silence except for some lusty smacking and deep breathing and then, looking at me slightly cross-eyed and a little drugged, he would say "wow!" No. Not just "wow." But: "W O W !!!!!" Otherwise he used sign language exclusively. Mainly with his tail. That could telegraph an enormous number of concerns. When he was in a loving mood, he would push his large head against my face, just once, and then walk away, with his tail saying, "That's enough. Let's not get mushy." In a way he was a mixture of a boor and a gentleman. Whenever we walked through a door together, he let me go first. He also was quite vain. He never passed a mirror without staring into it. When the cats in the nearby farm were in heat, I lost him. Sometimes he didn't come home for a whole week. The first time this happened, I was very worried. It was winter and the snow was very high and every black branch that stuck out of a snowdrift seemed to be his frozen paw. Then someone told me that they had seen him at the neighborhood farm, so I rushed over to see whether it was he. He was lying on some hay in the yard, stretched out voluptuously, a pasha lording it over a whole harem of delicious white and gray and multi-colored fluff rolling around him. When he saw me, he pretended not to know me. "Who are you?" he seemed to say. "Never saw you before." Then he got up and very slowly slinked into the barn, followed by all the fluff, and pausing just once, his tail said "Mother, go home. You embarrass me." I could not have been happier. All I wanted for him after all was a rich full life.

Mooky

Zizi died in the pursuit of love (or should I rather say sex). Following one of his amours across the road at night, he was hit by a car. I was very sad; we had been such good friends, and I thought he was indestructible. A week later I went to our local animal shelter, hoping that they might have an offspring of his. I was sure he had sired lots of them, all Burmese. But I was wrong. I was told, yes, they had a black male, but I wouldn't want him. "Nobody wants him," the lady said, "we have had him for three years, but we can't get rid of him." Can't get rid of him?!!! Of course I wanted to see him. And of course I took him home with me.

The first three days and nights he spent hiding behind the refrigerator. He didn't even come out for food. In the shelter he had lived in a cage four feet by five feet that was placed on top of boxes holding

Mooky

some young dogs. For three years!!! Small wonder that he was frightened of everything. But you should see him now. He owns my place! Obviously he is not a son of Zizi. He is black all right, but rather small and delicate, and there is quite a lot missing to make him a whole cat. I would say that I got about three-fourths of a cat when I took him home. He is declawed, has only one and a half ears, is of course altered, and has none of his small teeth which causes his food, dry or moist, forever to fall out of his mouth. But he is feisty and does not give up until he has eaten enough. He does have four very strong fangs that make him look a bit like a miniature hippo, and he has only four whiskers that ever so often fall out and are replaced in different locations. Athough he has none of Zizi's macho glitter, he is a real little guy with a lot of spunk, and a great need to show his affection. When I call him, he comes bounding through the meadow like a mountain goat and with the force of a bulldozer he rams his hard little head into my shoulder. Enough is never enough for him; he could go on forever.

The most outstanding thing about Mooky is that he seems not to be outstanding. Quite ordinary actually. But I think that is a disguise, because he is the most mysterious of all my cats. I know absolutely nothing about him, and he does not let me in on his secrets. Right now he is sitting next to the typewriter, looking very intently at me with his dark golden eyes, like copper plates, that one cannot penetrate. Little cat, who are you? Are you old, are you young? Did you have a good life before you came to the shelter? Have you been with a circus where you learned the somersaults I saw you attempt the other day? Sometimes when I talk to you, your eyes are glued to my lips as if you are trying to understand what I say. Then you look like a gifted young student with a scholarship. Are you a young student? Do you have a scholarship? Or did you belong to a witch and did you ride at Halloween on her broomstick? Because sometimes you do some very strange things. Like vanishing right in front of me or sleeping on the window sill and a moment later coming in from outdoors. All I know about you is that I don't know anything about you. Maybe we better just leave it that way. And no more silly questions!

The Dancing Hausfrau

Sometimes I have been tempted to call myself "the dancing Hausfrau." I love to cook. I love to bake. I love to have my friends share a meal with me. And of course I love to dance. But where is the connection between the two? Is there a similar joy involved in both? Or is it the success it can create? I really don't know. When my guests ask for a second – or third! – helping, I know I've done all right. But when I invent a new dance, I have no idea whether it is any good until I have performed it at least once. Not necessarily for an audience in a theater. It can be for just one person in a studio. But I need to bounce it off someone who has not seen it before. It seems that this gives me the distance I need to judge my own work. It does not mean at all that I must have approval; more important is that during the first showing I myself can agree with what I've done. It has happened several times that an audience accepted a new number, but I myself could not. Then it is better to take it out. Sometimes it can be mended, but not always. Or the opposite happens. An audience reacts poorly during a première, but I feel positive about it. Then I keep on doing it, at least until I have given it a chance to survive. When I did "The Artist in Person" for the first time in the Peppermill Program in Switzerland, there was no laughter at all from the audience and not one bit of applause at the end. This was quite disconcerting since the number is a satire, but I felt strongly that I should continue doing it. Later, it became the main reason that Voskovec and Werich asked me to join their Liberated Theater in Prague. It's all a bit of a mystery to me, including the fact that some of the best ideas for dances have come to me when I was cooking or baking. That sounds quite pedestrian, but it's true. Of course, comparisons can be very lopsided, but may be – after all – somewhere – there is a connection between a strudel and a tango.

Lotte Goslar's *Circus Scene*

by Joel Schechter, from his book *Durov's Pig*

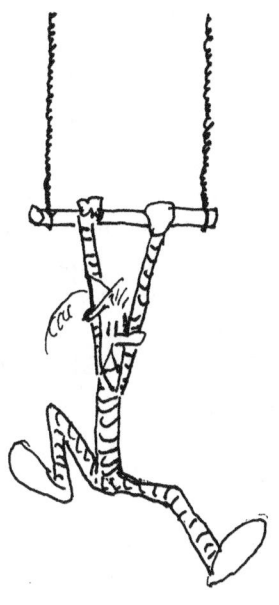

Lotte Goslar is a clown who dances. In her stage world a young ballerina refuses to obey her teacher; life-size toy soldiers shoot each other to music box accompaniment; a talent show contestant plays the violin with her feet; and a grandmother dances into heaven. Most of these comic scenes make no overt political statement, and Lotte Goslar does not think of herself as "a political person;" but during her fifty-year career she has performed in some of Europe's finest political cabarets. After permanently leaving Germany in 1933, at the age of sixteen, she danced comic solos as part of the Peppermill Revue, the anti-fascist cabaret show directed by Erika Mann, in tours across Europe. (The Peppermill subsequently served as a model for the cabaret featured in both the film and the play *Mephisto*, based on Klaus Mann's novel.) Goslar also performed with the Liberated Theatre, a satiric, anti-fascist group in Prague, before coming to New York with the Peppermill in 1938. There she continued to dance solo. In 1943 she joined the Turnabout Theatre in Hollywood and met Bertolt Brecht through their mutual acquaintances, Elsa Lanchester and Charles Laughton.

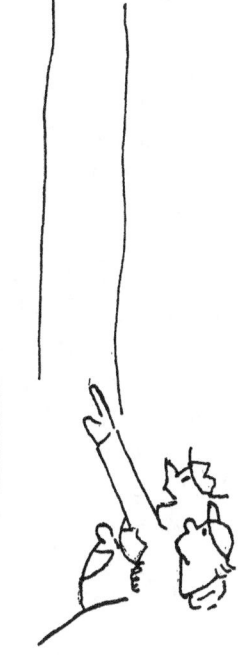

After Brecht saw one of Goslar's performances, he asked her to choreograph the carnival scene in his *Galileo*. This she did to his satisfaction in 1947. By her own account, she added one character to Brecht's play: in her interpretation, the street singers who mock Galileo through their ballads are joined by a hungry little girl who cannot dance. The singers have beaten the girl into learning some steps to illustrate their songs.

The tiny girl epitomizes the sort of reluctant dancer who still appears in Goslar's repertoire. Brecht liked her choreography of the street singing and carnival frolicking enough that he subsequently invited Goslar to become the Berliner Ensemble's choreographer in 1951. She declined the invitation, preferring to stay in the United States.

Goslar accepted another offering from Brecht, however. In 1947, without any prompting from her, he wrote a pantomine scenario for Goslar to perform, and dedicated it to her. The one-page scenario is still performed by her American company, Lotte Goslar's Pantomime Circus, a group which she formed in 1954 and which premiered at the Jacob's Pillow Dance Festival in Massachusetts. Goslar is the only artist who holds the rights to perform the scenario, which remains unpublished. When I discussed the scene with her at her country home in West Cornwall, Connecticut, in 1984, she graciously related the entire performance history of *Circus Scene*.

On paper, the scene reads almost like a parable by Franz Kafka. It describes "a much discussed scene of horror" which occurs "in a circus in A. [an unnamed city or country]." A clown is locked inside a cage with a lion. According to Goslar he is a "cheap little clown who entertains in between acts, and has fallen asleep." Once locked inside, he wakes, sees the lion and is mesmerized by its stare. The lion then compels the clown to perform tricks as if he (the clown) were a trained animal; the clown jumps upon platforms, balances on top of a ball and crawls up a ladder, under the direction of the paw-pounding lion. The scene ends when the spell is broken. The lion removes his eyes from the clown for a moment, and the clown, sensing his temporary freedom, jumps onto the lion and bites him to death. The murder of the lion is not a simple act of self-defense; Brecht's scenario suggests that the clown's rescue was near. Circus employees armed with pistols and iron hooks rush in just as the clown is killing the lion.

The scene is a curious example of Brecht's continuing interest in clowns. Smith, the clown in *The Baden Learning Play*, is far different from the nameless clown in *Circus Scene*. As discussed earlier, Smith is a passive victim, never resisting the torture inflicted on him. The transformation of an innocent clown into a fighter in *Circus Scene* is closer in tone to Brecht's *A Man's a Man*, in which the army turns the clownlike porter Galy Gay into a "human fighting machine." For this reason, James Lyon compares *A Man's a Man* to the later *Circus Scene* in his brief commentary on the scenario.

Brecht's scenario formed the basis for the pantomime, but Goslar added important elements not mentioned in the script at all: choreography, music, costumes and new characters – spectators who participate in the story by locking the clown in the cage and enjoying his predicament.

She also chose to divide the lion's role among four dancers, turning the animal into a collective character she compares to a "lynching party or Nazis."

The Men in the Lion Suit

Brecht himself was aware of something human about the lion – or something inhuman about the clown. As Goslar discovered in carefully studying Brecht's scenario, he refers to the clown as "the beast" ("Bestie") toward the end of the story. At first she thought that Brecht had made a mistake; but then she became convinced, with the advice of her friend, the German writer Hans Sahl, that Brecht meant it. The clown, in Brecht's own words, is transformed into the beast.

Goslar suggests the clown's transformation into a lion by having the clown take up and wield a whip which is worn as a tail by the lion until the closing moments. The whip-tailed lion is an abstraction, represented by four dancers, and it is primarily through the lion that Goslar demonstrates the affinity between man and beast. By dividing the role of the lion among four men and keeping the animal's human components quite visible, she suggests that a man can be part lion – if not wholly bestial. "I did not want a funny lion," Goslar declares. "I wanted it to be a powerful, dangerous unit." The four men "don't really look like a lion, but somehow convey an image of a lion. They [are] the front, the sides and the tail end – with a whip instead of a tail. There is a mane. A lion has only four legs, of course, and here were eight legs. So four of the legs [in the costumes Goslar designed] were yellow and the four meant to be invisible were black. When the lion is bitten by the clown, you see the four yellow legs [one on each dancer] move in a death agony." In this scene, as Brecht once said of epic acting, "there are no illusions that the player is identical with the character."

The Audience on the Stage

Although Lotte Goslar was given the circus scenario by Brecht in 1947, it was not publicly performed until 1972, at the ANTA Marathon Dance Festival in New York. The choreographer explains the delay this way:

> *For many years, I did not do anything with it. The main reason was the music. I totally work out of music. I never work with an idea first; music comes first, it has an atmosphere, suggests something vicious, or friendly or loving or ridiculous. And if I like the music, and I am induced to do something, some images come up. If they connect with the thoughts that I have had, it can become a number that also says something... I called Lotte Lenya [actress and widow of composer Kurt Weill, who wrote music for other Brecht texts] – years after I*

(a) Lotte Goslar performing *So What?* Photo: Otto Leib (b) Bertolt Brecht and Lotte Goslar discussing his *Galileo* in Los Angeles, 1947

had the script – and asked her whether Weill had any music not well known that I could use. She contacted the publisher, and they wrote her that there was one piece called "Café Royale." When I finally obtained it, the music was not at all what I wanted. Around the same period I heard another composition and I knew immediately that "this is the entire scene." It is by Mâche, and he composed it entirely with voices. You don't hear any real words. It sounds as if you are standing in the center of the circus ring and you hear the din of the voices, you hear laughter, screaming, shushing, everything, but it is just noise.

The voices represent the circus audience rather than the clown or lion. Goslar decided to give the audience a physical role in the piece as well as a vocal one. Brecht's scenario only twice refers to the spectators who "witness a strange happening" as they watch the lion gaze at the clown and tame him. Goslar gives form to the spectators' gazes as well as their voices, by placing performers onstage to represent the circus audience. They watch the scene of horror after one of their members initiates it, by locking the cage in which the clown has fallen asleep. Goslar recalls that she cast an audience in the scene, "because I am very much interested in human relations, what people do to each other, good or bad." She continues:

I know a lot of circus people, especially from the Ringling Brothers, and they have told me that when the aerialists work without a net they are paid time-and-a-half. I think that is an indictment of humanity; it means that more people will come to see the show when it is announced that there will be no net. I love to see the Chinese circus, where everybody is on a rope; they do the most fabulous things but you know they cannot get crushed in a fall.

So the spectators are sitting there and whenever the clown is in danger, this is what they want to see. Toward the middle of the scene, the clown is high up on the ladder and the lion has come apart, and two [parts of the lion] are climbing up, hitting [the clown]. It is almost as if [the clown] is doing a dance up there while trying to avoid being hit, and the spectators in the scene applaud. [None of this crowd reaction is mentioned in Brecht's outline]. The head of the lion goes up alone and gives the clown one last hit. The clown almost falls off but he is hanging there, dangling, and then his shoes come off and his pants come off and the [onstage] audience laughs, because they find it funny. I think Brecht would have liked this staging. At the very end, once the lion is dead, the clown steps over him and turns around to look at the onstage spectators who had tormented him. Now they are all afraid; now they all know it can happen to them. He steps forward, tears out the lion's tale (a whip), looks from one side to the other into the real audience and swings his whip as the light pins down his face.

The audiences onstage and off are linked by the clown's gaze in Goslar's production. These visual references to the audience, which she added to Brecht's outline, implement some of the playwright's own ideas about audience identification with onstage characters. Spectatorship, by its very nature, allows, applauds and gratefully accepts the torment of the clown.

Goslar says that the *spectators* torment the clown, it should be noted. They side with the lion; his gaze, which embodies a demand for thrills, and his enjoyment of the clown act, might be likened to theirs. "The whole thing is really a power game," adds Goslar.

There is a hint of what Wilhelm Reich has called "the mass psychology of fascism" hidden in Brecht's *Circus Scene*, and Goslar reveals it through her depiction of audience involvement. The mesmerizing gaze turns the clown into a slave and the lion into a spectator; and it might be the same gaze that Brecht had seen in the faces of "drugged" spectators for whom theatre is a narcotic. In his *Short Organon*, Brecht condemns such spells cast in the theatre, where spectators "look at the stage as if in a trance; an expression which comes from the Middle Ages, the days of witches and priests... These people seem relieved of activity, and like men to whom something is being done." Without recalling that Brecht wrote this, Goslar, too, compared the spectators in her *Clown Scene* to families in which parents carried children on their shoulders to see witch burnings. The trance described by Brecht in the *Short Organon* fits the passive state of the mesmerized circus clown. The clown's closing stares imply that his experience could become the spectators', and that they are potentially as vulnerable as he has been.

Although Brecht carefully avoids any explicit geographical or political references in his outline, and Goslar does the same in her choreography, it might be assumed that Brecht was writing about the predicament of those who would resist the spell and mass psychology of fascism; in order to defeat it, not only would they have to refuse its commands; they might also have to turn upon it with bestial force. James Lyon notes that late in Brecht's life the playwright "was fond of saying that in capitalistic society, if one fights a tiger, one becomes a tiger, i.e., that one assumes the characteristics of one's oppressors." *Circus Scene* certainly dramatizes this. It also suggests that dangerous spells can be cast in the world of art and showmanship, and in life, too.

Lotte Goslar has created many clowns in her life. She does not find the clown in *Circus Scene* particularly funny. "The whole scene is serious," she insists, adding that if it has a few funny moments, "they are only funny because the fear has been overemphasized. At one point, when the lion suddenly looks at the clown for the first time, the clown's reaction is one of fear. He wants to chase the lion away, so he runs toward him and tries to chase him; this always gets a laugh, and should, because it is futile." A clown scene with only a few laughs seems particularly appropriate for our bloodthirsty age, when we tend to encourage death-defying bravado, if not murder, in the circus as elsewhere.

From *Circus Scene*. The Clown (Danny Giagni) confronts the Lion (from left: Ray Collins, Bob Bowyer, Clay Taliaferro, Gary Easterling). Photo: John Lindquist

The Clown with a Whip

Goslar says she has been tempted to play the role of the clown in the scene herself, but has always felt "this should be played by a man. Most of the time for me a clown is an 'it,' a figure. In this case, the scene involves a man, who could have some strength against superstrength, the lion. A woman would be more vulnerable somehow." Few clowns have been less vulnerable than the one who holds the whip at the end of the Goslar/Brecht *Circus Scene*.

The ending Goslar devised for the scene has a curious antecedent in her own life, incidentally. She recalls that the Peppermill Revue never returned to Zurich after the Nazis disrupted a show there. Tear gas and clubbing filled the auditorium, while on stage the master of ceremonies, Erika Mann, stood alone. Mann was dressed as a stormtrooper but "in fairy tale terms," according to Goslar. The program was called "Fairy Tales," and the group had turned tales from Grimm and Andersen into satiric political commentaries. Mann's stormtrooper was dressed in a silver jacket, a parody of the Nazi look. Whip in hand, she stared outward while Swiss socialists fought the fascists in the theatre aisles. I suspect that during this battle Lotte Goslar first envisioned the clown with the whip, years before she relocated him in Brecht's *Circus Scene*.

The Lion from *Circus Scene*. From left: Clay Taliaferro, Gary Easterling, Bob Bowyer, Ray Collins, and Danny Giagni (as the clown). Photo: John Lindquist

TV

When I came to Hollywood in 1943 to dance at the Turnabout Theater, I was asked to participate in the pioneering experiments television station KTLA was conducting in Los Angeles. Those were really the infant days of television, and it is mindboggling to see the progress that has been made since.

Still, I believe that dance is probably the most difficult art form to translate to the screen. And I also know that my particular kind of performance poses additional problems. In the theater I, as the choreographer, can, without its knowing, force an audience to focus on any part of the stage I want it to. On camera that would translate into the constant use and change of close-ups and long shots – sometimes in rapid succession. It would require a good amount of time to acquaint the director and the camera crew with the variations within a single number. They would have to "learn" the dance. On our many tours in Europe and the USA, that was out of the question, especially in the sixties and seventies, when almost all of our TV appearances were shot the same day as our performance in a given town. These stations had a minimal budget and often, as director, a fledgling newcomer who had been told never to go overtime. He invariably looked at our numbers just once and our desperate questions were all answered with "don't worry," "I'll fix it," "trust me," and – to finally calm us down – "you're great." It so reminds me of Fellini's film "Ginger and Fred." There seemed to be a general belief that we dancers may be competent on stage but that we definitely need to have our work improved for television.

I know what I am talking about. In Europe we were under the management of the impresario Ernst Krauss the same as Susanna and José, the famous Spanish dance team. We often watched each other's TV shows. One of their most successful numbers was a Zapateado, in which they were seen in one spot on stage, passionately close together, with their torsos stretched high and totally still, while their feet did a fantastic, rapid, staccato tremolo and their eyes were shooting daggers and flames. This ominous stillness of the bodies together with the fury of the feet is what a Zapateado is all about. It's the dancers' footwork that makes the theaters ring with olés. But leave it to the underpaid imagination of the fledgling director. Here he comes ready to "improve" in three minutes what Susanna and José had built up in endless rehearsals. All you saw during the entire number were the faces of the two in close-up. Even with superhuman effort they could not avoid an infinitely slight trembling of their heads, as their feet were stamping the ground. But not for even a second did the screen show the tremendous fireworks of their feet. All one saw of the two brilliant young dancers were their hugely enlarged faces seemingly tottering from a nervous breakdown and steeped in sweat and agony. Olé!

Magic

The stage is magic! If you believe in what you do and if you have fully prepared yourself, you can be anything for your audience. You can be old or young, tall or short, heavy or slim, beautiful or ugly, no matter how you look in reality. You can die or evaporate or be born right in front of your audiences and they will believe it. Or you can be an animal or a stone or a large group of people or a house or the moon, full or crescent. There is absolutely no limit. But one thing is essential. You must never lose yourself in the character you portray. You should never assume that you *are* the person or the creature or the thing you play. All you can do is tell about it – 100% of course, but you should not try to identify yourself with it. You would be fooling yourself if you thought you could. Let's assume you were playing a cow. You will never look like one, but you can tell so convincingly about "cow," even without a special costume, that the audience will not see *you* any more, but a cow in the meadow with a tail and horns. Magic! I once saw Danny Kaye being a slot machine, and I did not see a young man in a suit standing on a stage. I saw a slot machine. I saw the penny he inserted; I saw a display of lights; I heard the inner workings of the instrument, and I saw the penny falling out again. And all the time Danny had done almost nothing. What he *had* done was this: he had found the very essence of the situation and he had pared it down to the least action. That is one of the most important, and often most difficult, things to achieve: simplicity! To edit one's own work rigorously, no matter how fond one is of a detail. But the result is usually worth the agony.

One more reason you should not get lost in a part is that all the time you are on stage, you have to be aware – and if necessary in control – of a lot of things: the shape and size of the stage itself; the lights; the wings; the sets and props; the costumes; the floor; your partners and so much more. This awareness, this margin of control will not diminish the richness of your performance, if you treat if right. It is not more than the peripheral view of your eyes that accompanies your focus. You still can create all the magic in the world. And what if something goes wrong? Your zipper breaks, your skirt slips, your taped music fades out? Those things do happen. But you will want, or even have, to go on. And although some of the disasters cannot be solved easily, it will help if you are in control.

Not So Magic

Like every performer, I have been through a few good disasters myself. All I could do then was try to compensate by giving an especially strong performance, stressing all the positive points and hoping that the audience would forget the mishap. I particularly remember a number called "First Dance," a rather poetic piece in which I portray my mother dancing with me as a three-year-old child. I am dressed in an old-fashioned long skirt and a lacey blouse. The dance starts with me backing out of one of the wings, slightly bent over, leading the imaginary little girl in her first shy dancing steps. The trouble was that just before this number I had done one of my clown dances, and in the great rush backstage, I had forgotten to take off the huge green clown's shoes. I realized it only when I was in full view of the audience. It was too late to do anything about it but try to compensate and hope for the best.

Another time, at the International Dance Festival in Aix-les-Bains, I performed a number called "Conversation with an Ant" in which I, sitting in a garden chair, pick up an imaginary ant from the grass and talk to her, to convince her that there is no sense in rushing about. The ant agrees and walks slowly away. But when we sent the program to the festival to be translated into French, the editor could not believe that "ant" was what we really meant and printed the French word for "aunt" instead. "Conversation avec une tante" (Conversation with an aunt) was what the audience read in the program. They wondered why I was looking at my finger all through the number, when I was just talking to my aunt. Of course this situation could have been solved by an announcement over a loudspeaker, but the trouble was that I didn't know about the mistake. Until later.

Of course there are some problems that simply cannot be solved at all. Luckily, in my long dancing life I've only had to cancel a performance once. I was dancing in a musical in New York and for an off-weekend I had accepted an engagement at one of the popular summer camp resorts in the Catskill mountains in New York State. There was a large outdoor stage, and I was to dance the three numbers from the New York show, one of which was a take-off on chorus girls. When I arrived for the dress rehearsal, I found the stage to be very slippery because it had

Lotte Goslar in *Conversation with an Ant*. Photo: Particam

rained for the whole previous week. The downpour had stopped and the forecast for the next day was good.

Unfortunately, however, no one from the hotel had noticed that the piano, an upright, had been left standing all the time on that outdoor stage, not only uncovered but also with both its lids wide open. By now it was filled with enough water to make a couple of goldfish happy. What to do? First of course we asked the manager whether there was another instrument on the premises, only to hear that they had a baby grand, but that it had lost two of its legs and most of the black keys. "Not to worry," the manager said and called for an army of hefty cleaning women brandishing mops and sponges to soak up the flood. "It's all yours now," he announced with a smile. "Not to worry."

But soon we knew that we had a lot to worry about. The music for the Chorus Girl number is a demanding virtuoso arrangement by Benny Goodman of "Tiger Rag", and I had permission to use the piano version that I think his brother had made. The trouble was that the first key my pianist punched down refused to come up again. And so did the next and the next and the next. And eventually they all just stayed down. The felts on each hammer had swollen so much from the weeklong deluge that we would have needed a large group of people standing close around the piano to pull each hammer up again the moment my pianist had depressed it. And that is exactly what we tried to do.

Only it didn't work. "Tiger Rag" is a very fast piece, and what the young waiters who volunteered managed to accomplish had the speed of a dirge and of course none of the rhythm of ragtime. So we quickly vetoed this brilliant idea. In the meantime a large number of weekend guests who had heard our loud rescue attempts came rushing to our stage to hear and see everything first hand and to tell us exactly what to do next. The majority thought that heated electric blankets were the answer. The blankets were located quickly, but not the extension cords needed to connect them to the piano on the faraway stage. Gloom descended over the Catskills. But not for long. Because who was coming down the garden path but good old Johnny, the entertainment director of the camp who was in charge of making everyone happy during the summer months. Why didn't anybody think of him before? Of course he would come up with the right solution. And so he did. "What do you do," asked Johnny, "when a baby wets the diaper?... You use baby powder!"

And that's how it all ended. The baby powder was rushed to the stage. The confident entertainment director poured it all – two big containers of it – on the swollen wet felts, and the hammers were glued together for the rest of their natural life.

And there was no performance by L. G.

A New Experience

To work with the dancer Martha Clarke on her *Vienna/Lusthaus* has been an unusual experience. I have been an admirer of hers for many years, starting with her "Pilobolus" days, and she likes what I do. Several times we have discussed collaboration on some future project. So far this has not happened, except that in the summer of 1984 (each of us doing her own stuff), we shared a program at the Lenox Arts Center in Massachusetts. In the meantime I joined her *Vienna/Lusthaus* production, and that is where the "unusual experience" started. Unusual? That's not the right word. Totally uprooting is more like it. I had never in my life been directed by anyone except in some videos and in the very beginning of my dancing life by Palucca. After that I was always on my own, either as a solo performer or since 1954 with my own company, the Pantomime Circus. I could not have chosen a more extraordinary, engrossing and disturbing experience than working with Martha. First of all, I think she has a stroke of divine madness that is harnessed by her total professionalism, her total involvement, her unbelievable energy, and her almost somnambulistic way of finding the right footing on the tightrope walk across the abyss of her fantasy.

Sometimes this is maddening: her almost compulsive way of not only changing, but destroying her best inventions, turning things upside down without any seeming reason or logic – but lo and behold, after having gone with her through that near-chaotic process again and again, after being exhausted and sometimes even furious about it all, you have to admit she has been right. She had shaken up all the ingredients and smashed all the particles. In the process the nuggets have separated from the residue. She had a vision all the time, which she could not sufficiently articulate, even to herself. But like a sleepwalker, she arrived after all. I don't think she will ever fall down from the roof she is climbing. That means that during rehearsals one is alternately enchanted by her world or totally frustrated. Twice I asked her to release me. She asked me to be patient, to trust her. I could not agree with her at first, but I'm glad I finally did. It has given me a lot of new experience. Aside from that, she is one of the most considerate, friendly and patient people I know in this profession, very, very hard-working, vulnerable, and always between despair and delight. A child possessed by a demon.

Marilyn

I'm often asked how well I knew Marilyn Monroe. She was a student of mine in Hollywood in the late forties and we soon became friends. But I cannot say that I knew her. Did she know herself, I often wondered? Sometimes I even felt sorry for her. She was caught in the cruel and relentless treadmill of fame and stardom without being quite able to overcome that menace. She had so much more to offer than merely being a sex goddess, such clear recognition of quality. I liked her and I liked her considerable talents, especially her sense of humor. I thought that later in life she might follow in the footsteps of a Mae West. Many of her films show how capable she was of spoofing her own sex appeal. But what impressed me most were the small and very telling human touches that showed up all the time. I had been told by my colleagues at the Turnabout Theater that Marilyn Monroe came every week with her young agent to see all four of our programs. I think that was during the shooting of her film *The Seven Year Itch*. And soon she called me, not by way of a secretary as several starlets had done, but announcing herself in her wispy voice simply with, "This is Marilyn."

Initially she asked for private lessons, but I thought it would be better for her to be in a class of "regular" young people and not to rest on the pedestal of her fame. I had assembled a group of gifted actors and dancers as possible future members of my company. She joined and turned out to be an outstanding student, full of imagination and very eager to accept my criticisms, especially when I warned her that any over-display of her natural sexy qualities could only lead to parody. In contrast to her legendary lateness on the film sets, she was always on time for our two weekly sessions. Obviously she liked to come; she was happy to be with us as a student, rather than as a star on display. Relaxed and without fears, barefoot, in jeans, with tousled hair and without any makeup, she looked her most beautiful. The natural bone structure of her face was exquisite and her hands always made me think of medieval wood sculpture. Amazing and really touching was her modesty. Whenever I said something encouraging to her, tears would well up in her eyes. How I wished I could have helped her more, but there simply wasn't enough time. My marriage and the work with my company and the Turnabout were truly all-consuming.

Of course I went as often as I could when she asked me to come and watch her filming, but I must confess that I felt uneasy when after every "take" she rushed to me to get my comments. When I told George Cukor of my concern, he urged me to come as often as I could. "It helps me," he said. "She relaxes when you are here." How frightened, how insecure she must have been!

What do I remember most about Marilyn? The people who worked with her often told me that she was extremely generous; I found this generosity expressing itself in many different ways: in compassion, in concern, and in kindness. No matter where she or I were at that time, she always called me on December 24 – the German Christmas, but also the day my husband had died. She never mentioned what had happened on that day, but simply let me know that there was a friend thinking of me. When one of the students in our class was inducted into the army, she took him out for lunch on his last day with us. All of this seems small, but to me it reveals a lot. And so does this: I was visiting Marilyn and her husband, Arthur Miller in Connecticut in the house they had just bought. She was leaning over a mangy-looking geranium that she told me she had found dying but had rescued. She had just discovered that a single tiny fresh leaf had sprouted out of the sick mess. She was euphoric!

Small stuff all of that, one might think, but to me it signals something else. Marilyn seemed constantly to confront the question "Where do I belong?", small wonder when you realize that as a child and young adult she had been in so many different foster homes! Do I think she killed herself? No, I don't. I rather believe that she was careless with her life, which is dangerously close to suicide. When I talked to her a few days earlier, she had just come back from a trip to Mexico where she had bought all sorts of things for her modest new house – the first one she ever owned – pots and pans and tiles for ceiling and floors, all of it cheerful in the Mexican tradition. She seemed to be in very good spirits. But only God knows.

Joe DiMaggio, who even after their divorce had remained a caring friend, made the arrangements for her funeral. Only a very small group was invited: her much-revered acting teacher Lee Strasberg and his wife; one of her directors; her hairdresser; a few studio workers; her lawyer; her secretary and me. We all had been at the simple service in the adjacent chapel and now we were standing in front of the vault. In our different ways, we all had loved that girl who had slipped away without warning.

The stone walls surrounding the cemetery were lined by a large crowd of strangers who had come to see the "show." It was a sunny California day, and everyone was dressed in gay slacks and shirts. There was some murmuring and some shouting, even some laughter and the sound of transistor radios. It was like a picnic. Some handsome young police guards (or were they extras for tomorrow's soap opera?) took care that nobody would came close to the tremendous mountain of flowers from all over the world, piled high in front of the vault. And that box – if only that box weren't there. Then some people in black lifted that box and pushed it into the slot that said "Marilyn Monroe," one of the loveliest and maybe one of the most unhappy human beings in the world.

We left soon after. So did the police, as the entire crowd from the stone walls descended in one big wave, tearing every single flower off that huge mountain. Not one flower was left. Maybe Marilyn would have liked that, just as she loved the adoration of thousands of soldiers when she entertained at military camps. It may have told her that she was beloved by the whole world. But I think she was confused. What she needed was less adoration, and more of what is real.

Hans and Ute Sahl, April, 1992, Berlin at the George Grosz-Platz, Kurfürstendamm, Berlin

A Large Landscape

December 1992: Today I got a video tape about Hans Sahl, my beloved friend of more than fifty years. On the cover is a picture of his face as he looks now. But it's not just a face – it's a landscape. This landscape wears a jaunty cap and horn-rimmed glasses and his trademark: a fire-red scarf, not unlike the one Aristide Bruant wears in the portrait by Toulouse-Lautrec. The photo is black and white, but I know that the scarf is fire-red, because it had been mine before he borrowed it and then could not give it back.

The most remarkable part of the landscape is his eyes. Although he is almost totally blind, they look at you with so much life that it is difficult to realize that he can hardly see anything. What he receives from them is minimal, but what he translates it into is enormous. They are like pieces of sky or like small lakes, that change with the weather of his mind. There are sunny and rainy times. There is wisdom and sometimes anger. And very often understanding and deep concern. His eyes don't lie. I often wonder whether he knows how much they tell.

All the planes of his face, his cheeks and chin for instance, all the wrinkles and crevices are like mountains and valleys that speak of a long and perilous journey through life; much sorrow and despair, many lost hopes, but also much strength and stubbornness and an unending joy in living with all his senses. And his humor!!!!! That devilish humor of his! Even before his mind forms one of his witty remarks, his mouth announces it. Two dimples appear in his cheeks and around his lips it looks like lightning. It blinks and winks and twinkles, almost as if he is pre-tasting the *bon mot* that lurks in his mind. And of course there is no holding it back any longer.

There are also some dark and permanent canyons in this landscape, deep grooves that lead from his nose to his chin, that tell of the years and years of frustrations and loneliness. But all of that is topped by his beautiful, very high forehead, the seat of all his thoughts and fantasies. It's a very rich, clear and uncluttered part of his landscape. Nothing is twisted, nothing is hidden. It tells the truth, no matter how dangerous the truth has often been for him.

What's So Funny?

When I first saw the wonderful drawing of "Yes" and "No" by Saul Steinberg, one of my favorite artists, I thought: This is the essence of all fools. Here, in a few lines, was "Yes," the soul of the clown, portrayed as a silly, tinkly and vulnerable vehicle on ridiculous, impractical wheels. Sporting a cheerful little flag and armed with outlandish gadgets, "Yes" moves confidently into battle against the horrible monster "No," a fortress merciless and strong, brutal and invincible – a stupid and eternal power.

"Yes" does not have a chance in the world. I thought he would be crushed, destroyed in no time. We know this for sure. And yet in the face of all logic and sanity, on a level beyond reasoning, we also know he can win. It is David and Goliath all over again. The little bells of "Yes's" foolish optimism will drown out "No's" awesome roar.

Of course, to anyone with a sober mind this is sheer lunacy. This clown is crazy! He is an optimist! An optimist in this day and age! Has he seen the cracks in the wall? Does he know that this bombastic monster is made of papier-maché, that he is hollow? No, I'm afraid it is not quite that easy. This wall is every bit as strong and horrible as it seems and the clown knows it. He may be a fool but he is nobody's fool.

What then gives him his insane courage? What right, what nerve, does the clown have in our time to tinkle the bells of his optimism? In view of wholesale brutality and injustice, with more and more true values toppling and false ones rising, in full view of agony and endless misunderstanding, shouldn't the clown stop being funny and instead scream in outrage? Is he not merely naive and callous in his insistence on laughter?

Compassion is largely a matter of imagination. It is the artist, then, and certainly the clown, who should be most capable of compassion. How can he insist on his funny turns when the whole world is on fire? There is only one answer: He is born with his bells. His optimism and courage are his weapons.

To be funny, that is, to bring joy, one has to be capable of experiencing at least a measure of joy oneself. Not happiness necessarily – that might be asking too much – but joy. It simply will not do to be bitter and tense. At times you feel like saying: "Excuse me, sir, I'm terribly sorry, but I believe that there is, once in a while, some reason for joy left in this admittedly difficult world. Do you mind?"

Because, odd as it may seem, Love, Friendship, Decency, Courage and Beauty still exist. Even today. The supply may be alarmingly short, but it simply would not be true to deny them altogether – just as it would be invalid to doubt the vast supplies of hate, greed, hypocrisy and "couldn't-care-less-ness." It still makes sense to pursue the one and fight the other. But to fight, you have to be an optimist. For instance, a clown.

Solos

Intoxication. Photo: Constantine

Lotte Goslar in *The Life of a Flower*. Photo: Larry Frost

Lotte Goslar in *Grande Tristesse*. Photo: Otto Leib

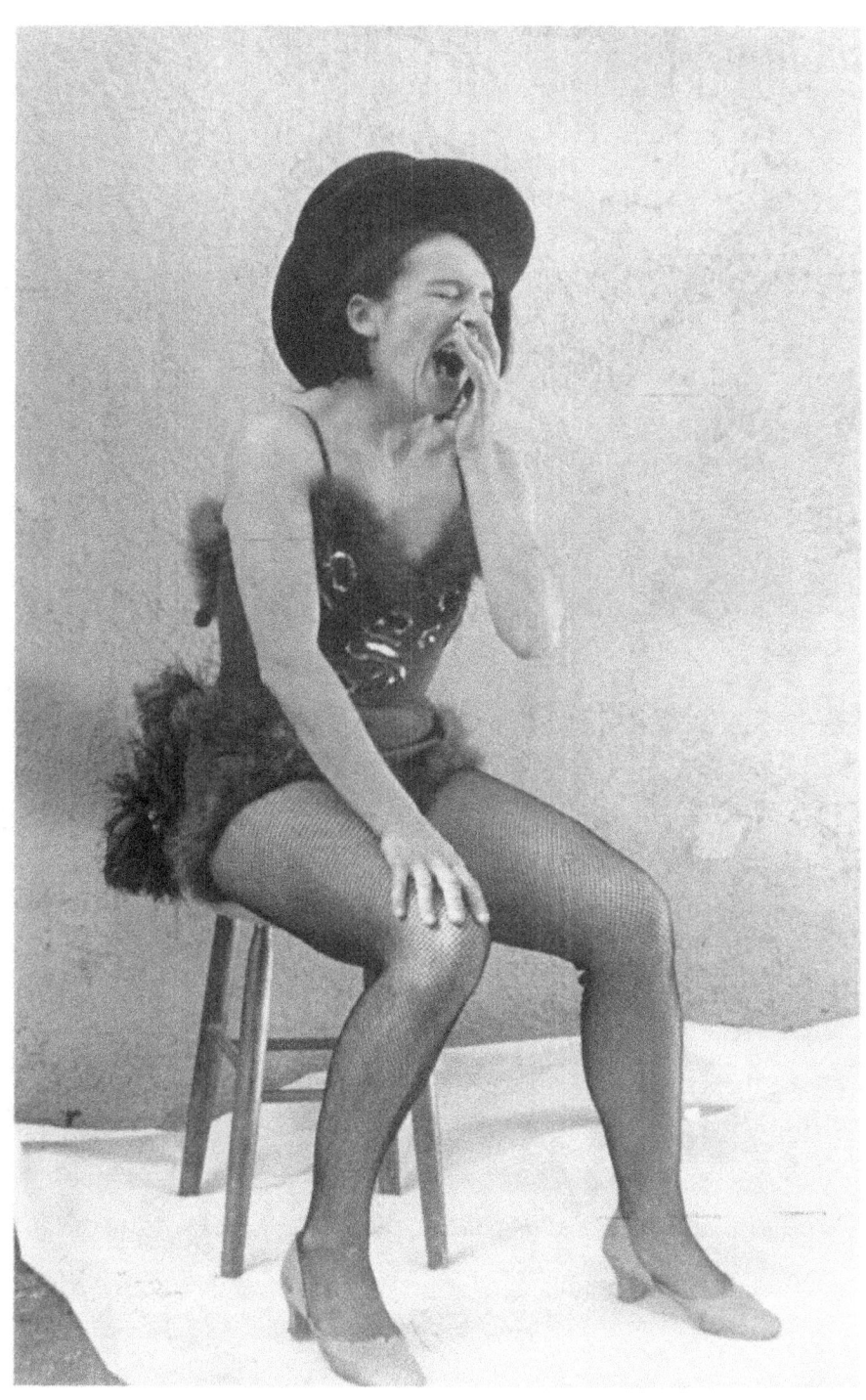

Lotte Goslar in *Midnight Show*, Hollywood 1944. Photo: Gerda

Lotte Goslar as the Child in *Grandma Always Danced*. Photo: ASMP Globe

Lotte Goslar in *Grandma Always Danced*. Photo: ASMP Globe

Lotte Goslar in *Grandma Always Danced*. Photo: ASMP Globe

Lotte Goslar in *A Guardian Angel*. Photo: Constantine

Lotte Goslar in *Cheap Clown – Not Wanted*. Photo: Potter B. Hueth

Lotte Goslar in *Gift Wrapped*. Photo: Constantine

The Company

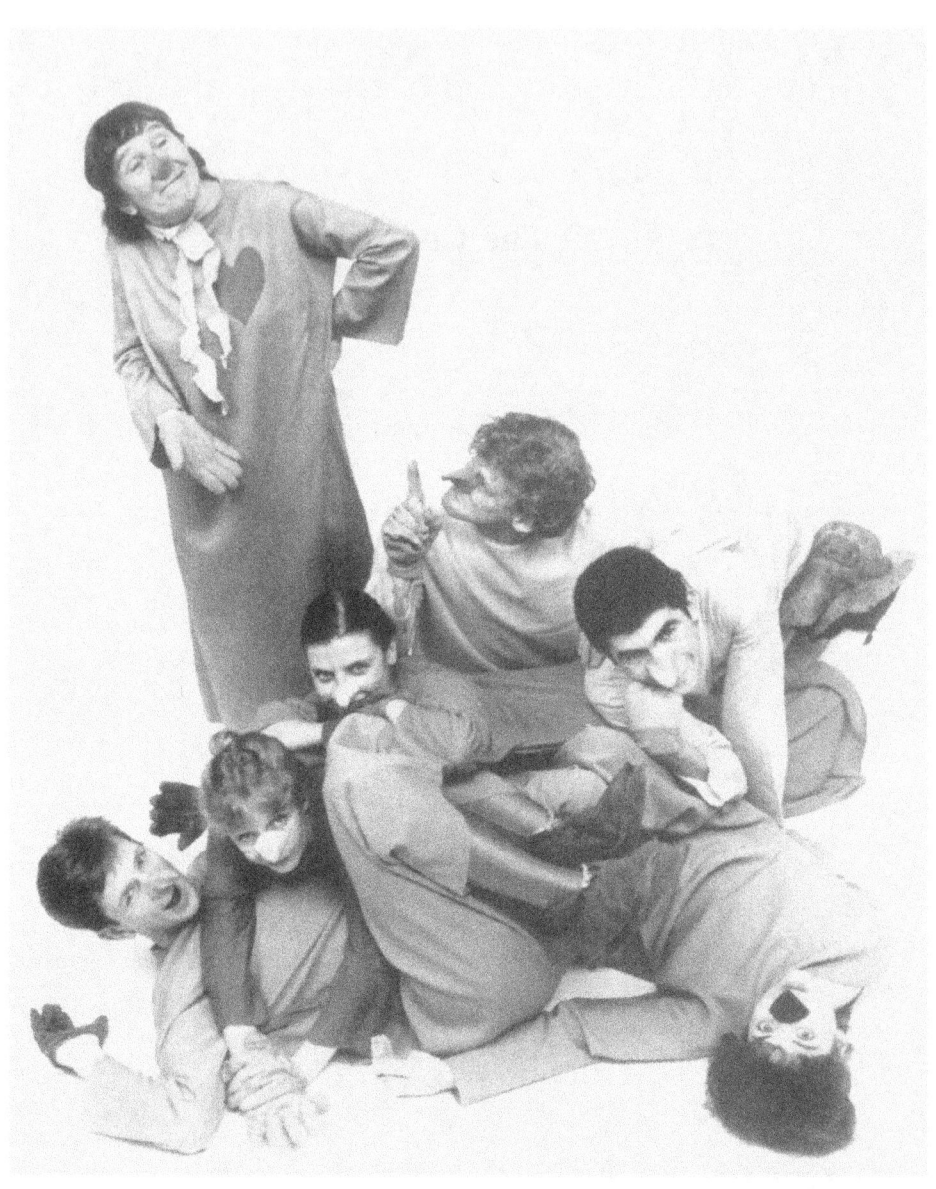

Lotte Goslar and The Company in *Greetings*. From left: Gene French, Kathleen Carlin, Lotte Goslar, Stephanie Godino, Lance Westergard, Algul Gamma, Janis Roswick. Photo: Jessica Katz

The Pantomime Circus in *Pink Waltzes*. From left: Kathleen Carlin, Charles Haack, Janis Roswick, Gene French, Stephanie Godino, Lance Westergard. Photo: Schmid

Lou Zeldis and Kathleen Carlin in *Infatuation*. Photo: John Lindquist

Lotte Goslar, Lance Westergard and Algul Gamma in *Hello! Hello?* Photo: Jessica Katz

Lotte Goslar's *Talent Show*. From left: Kathleen Carlin, Mary Gambardella and Janis Roswick. Photo: John Lindquist

Lotte Goslar and Jess Meeker in *Liebestraum*. Photo: John Lindquist

Letters

Zu einer viel diskutierten Schreckensszene kam es in einem Zirkus in A., als ein Clown durch ein technisches Versehen in den Löwenzwinger geriet. Aus Todesfurcht vollführte der Mann, um den Löwen einzuschüchtern, einige gewalttätigen Bewegungen herrischer Art. Die Zuschauer erlebten hierauf ein seltsames Ereignis Geschehnis. Sie sahen, wie der Löwe, in die Käfigmitte trabend, den Clown zu fixieren begann und bald dazu überging, ihn nach allen Regeln der Kunst zu bändigen. Mit ruhigen, aber machtvollen Tatzenschlägen auf den Holzmehlbestreuten Boden bedeutete er dem völlig gebannten Clown seine Intentionen, liess ihn auf die kleinen runden Podeste hopsen, auf einem Ball balanzieren, über eine vergrösserte Hennenleiter kriechen usw usw. Dann ereignete sich der erwähnte Unfall. Aus irgend einem Grund wandte der Löwe seinen Blick von der Bestie und diese, eben ziemlich hoch auf der Leiter balanzierend, gewann mit einem wilden Sprung den Boden, stürzte sich auf den unglücklichen Löwen und machte sich, der herbeilaufenden, Pistolen abschiessenden und mit eisernen Hacken nach ihm fuchtelnden Angestellten nicht achtend, daran, ihn totzubeissen.

(Lotte Goslar gewidmet)   Brecht

Bertolt Brecht's *Aus dem Zirkusleben* (*From Life in the Circus*). Copyright © by Stefan S. Brecht 1997 and 1998. All rights reserved by Suhrkamp Verlag Frankfurt am Main.

(subject for a pantomime?)

From t~~he~~ life in the Circus

A much discussed scene of horror occured in a Circus in A.,
when, because of a technical error, a Clown got inside the Lion's
cage. Scared to death and in order to intimidate the Lion, the man
executed several violent movements of an imperious kind. Whereupon
the spectators witnessed a strange happening. They saw how the
Lion, trotting to the center of the cage, started to gaze at the
Clown and how he soon proceeded to tame him mercilessly. With
calm but powerful blows of his paws on the sawdust covered floor,
he made his intentions known to the totally mesmerized Clown, let
him hop on the small round pedestals, balance on top of a ball,
crawl over an enlarged chicken ladder, etc. etc. Then, the
aforementioned accident happened. For some unknown reason, the
Lion averted his gaze from the beast and he, just balancing
rather high on the ladder, reached the floor with one wild leap,
plunged himself upon the unlucky Lion and proceeded —without
heeding the employees who rushed in shooting their pistols
and fidgeting their iron hooks — to bite him to death.

(Dedicated to Lotte Goslar)   Brecht

BERTOLT BRECHT   Berlin, 12. März 1951

Liebe Goslar,

ich sprach heute mit Therese Giehse, die bei uns im "Berliner Ensemble" gastiert, darüber, wie gut es wäre, Sie hier zu haben. Nicht nur im Berliner Staatstheater und in der Komischen Oper Felsensteins, auch bei uns im Berliner Ensemble wären Sie sehr wichtig. (U.a. planen wir auch wieder den Galileo Galilei). Das ist natürlich alles im Ostsektor Berlins und vielleicht macht das die Sache für Sie schwierig. Aber wenn Sie auch nur im geringsten Interesse daran haben, wären Sie sehr willkommen.

                            Herzlich Ihr

Sehen Sie noch Else und Charles? Bitte grüssen Sie sie von Helli und mir nachdrücklichst.

BERLIN-WEISSENSEE, BERLINER ALLEE 190, FERNRUF 560393 . BANK: BERLINER STADTKONTOR 20/94134
BERLIN NW 7, LUISENSTRASSE 18, FERNRUF 421968 (BERLINER ENSEMBLE)

Letter to Lotte Goslar from Bertolt Brecht, Berlin, 12 March 1951. Copyright © by Stefan S. Brecht 1997 and 1998. All rights reserved by Suhrkamp Verlag Frankfurt am Main.

Bertolt Brecht   Berlin, 12. March 1951

   Dear Goslar,

   today I talked with Therese Giehse, who is a guest performer
   with us at the "Berliner Ensemble", about how good it
   would be to have you here. Not only in the Berliner
   Staatstheater (Berlin Municipal Theater) and in t̶h̶e̶
   Felsenstein's Komischer Oper (Comic Opera), but also
   with us in the **Berliner** Ensemble you would be very important.
   (Among others we also plan again the Galileo Galilei) .
   Of course all of that is in the East sector of Berlin
   and maybe that makes the matter difficult for you.
   But if you have even only the slightest interest in it,
   you would be very welcome.

                    Heartily (or cordially)

                                        Brecht

   Are you still seeing Elsa and Charles? Please give them
   the most emphatic regards from Helli and me.

AGNES GEORGE DE MILLE

25 East 9th Street
New York 3
December 31, 1947

Dear Lotte:

I saw "Galileo" the other night and was knocked flat out of my seat into the aisle by the marvellous setting you gave the song in Act II. It is really very wonderful and has all of your best quality, ironic, dirty, tender, frightening and in some awful way amusing. It reminded me of Hogarth and Breughel, two people you probably never heard of.

My husband who is Sol Hurok's assistant was enchanted. I have been telling him steadily with the persistence of water wearing away rock that you should be given a tour with your people. Of course, they cannot negotiate anything like that without having seen you. What are the chances of your coming to New York for a recital? I wish you could manage this. I think the time is ripe. Kreutzberg has had a remarkably successful tour on his return.

I get wild entreating letters from Rosalind de Mille. I have never seen her dance and have no idea of her capabilities. How good is she and what can she do? The photographs she has sent me indicate a rather dubious ballet technique but that of course is not of essential importance. Is she a good comedienne as she suggests?

Happy New Year to you, Lotte. It is fine to see some glimpse of your work again. I have missed it. Incidentally the program credit was very confusing. Many people thought you had trained McKracken, arranged her runnings around and faintings, etc. If there is a repeat performance see that you get credit for that particular song and call it by name.

Yours with affection

Agnes
(Mrs. Walter Prude)

From Agnes de Mille, December 31, 1947. With the kind permission of Professor Jonathan Prude.

AGNES GEORGE DE MILLE

25 East 9th Street
New York City 3
January 28, 1948

Dear Lotte:

Your letter distressed me dreadfully. It is very hard for me to know what to say except for God's sake hold on, don't give up. You are a remarkable artist – there is nobody like you and whenever your work is brought in contact with an intelligent public the result is terrific. I am sorry that Mr. Hurok did not fire. He is a dear old man but he has very little perception except for what is brilliant in technical performance and flamboyant in style. Tschaikowsky is his favorite musician and Scheherazade is his favorite ballet. It is with sad reluctance that he has accepted Tudor, Balanchine, Robbins and me as here to stay and for the life of him he cannot explain it. Walter, on the other hand, has sense and had he been along things might have been different. But anyhow Hurok caters to a large submerged public whose sea level is considerably lowered by the community concert groups. These are so far beneath an alert theater audience that I don't think they could sit through a performance from start to end of any of the better Broadway plays. They represent the neighborhood moving picture house intelligence and Hurok may be right. They wouldn't either understand or like you. What you need is an intelligent theater public and maybe that will come by getting on Broadway or meeting an intelligent moving picture director. All you need is proper presentation. I shall think about this very carefully.

It is very sad that our greatest artists have such a difficult time. Graham is always struggling but Graham is esoteric and appeals only to the highest intelligence. That naturally limits her audience radically. Carmelita is extremely neurotic and is constantly thwarting every effort to help her. I know what I am talking about. I have long been one of the thwartees. Doris Humphreys cannot adapt her style either to the theater or ballet groups. I think you can. There is generally a real and practical reason why people do not get on – I mean when they have great and unusual talent. Please do not despair. When I have thought a bit I will write again.

Affectionately
Agnes

From Agnes de Mille, January 28, 1948. With the kind permission of Professor Jonathan Prude.

January 16, 1981

Dear Ms. Goslar:

The performance you and your company gave on December 23 at the "Y" provided me with one of the richest and most exciting theatrical experiences in my memory. I had seen you perform in Central Park fifteen or more years ago and have never forgotten that pleasure. Ever since then I've looked forward to seeing you again – you were worth the wait!

The most profound moment of the evening came with the performance of the "Circus Scene." Enclosed is a poem, in letter form, which was written about that dance.

Sincerely,

Renée Felice

From Renée Felice, January 16, 1981

TO THE ATTENTION OF THE RINGMASTER

Esteemed Sir,

This is a warning that *cannot*, for the welfare of all who come under your aegis, *be taken too seriously!*

Regarding Your Clowns!

Take the utmost care to provide them with lavish attention. *No expense should be spared* to supply them with the highest quality greasepaint, the most durable costumes, the most reliable properties. *Choose personally* the tastiest morsels for their table and *do not fail* to keep their quarters amply heated in winter, cool in summer. *Tenderly minister* to their health and *earnestly endeavour* to provide them with diversion.

Above all, I pray you, *pay the utmost attention* to the following instruction: *KEEP YOUR CLOWNS AT THE FARTHEST POSSIBLE DISTANCE FROM THE LIONS!*

Should you fail in this, notwithstanding scrupulous attention to the above-suggested particulars, the danger exists that *the Clowns may descend upon* and *devour the Lions.*

Yours, in earnest devotion,

A Concerned Citizen

From a concerned citizen – undated

I love you thousand.

                                        Peter (5 years old)

                    A Fan Letter – undated

Lotte Goslar with Joseph Papp and Bernard Gersten, discussing the forthcoming Children's Shows at the Delacorte Theater in New York, circa 1965

List of Works

Dances created in Germany before 1933, all Solos	Composer
The Disgruntled	Casella/Goslar
The Spinster	folk/Wagner
The Woodsprite	folk
Femme Fatale	Paganini
The So-What	Goslar
Little Circus Dancer	Goslar
Noli me tangere	trad. polka

Dances created in Europe, outside Germany, between 1933 and 1937, all Solos	
Lento	Bartok
Young Mother	Jezek
Fille de Joie	Jezek
Intoxication	Jezek
Cupid I	Lange
Chorus Girl I	B. Goodman, "Tiger Rag"
Little Heap of Misery	McCoy
Suite Feminine	Couperin, Lully
The Hero	trad. marches
Prima Ballerina	Strauss/Gounod
Guardian Angel	music arrangement
The Artist Himself	Goslar
Daily Dozen	jazz potpourri

Dances created in America, since 1937
(Solo: S, Duet: D, Trio: T, Quartet: Q, Company: Co.)
When cast includes L. Goslar, a "G" is added

Petite Valse, D	Lanner
Waltzmania, S G	Strauss
Gift Wrapped, S G	Lange

First Dance, S G	folksongs
Like a Bird, S	Milhaud
Conversation with an Ant, S G	Chopin
Dog Act, S G	Stravinsky
Grandma Always Danced, S G	German folk
The Pooh-to-you, S G	polka
Bitter Dreams, Co	Bartok
Come, Sweet Death, S G	Bach
Old Clown, S G	Stravinsky
No Waltz, D	P. Gilbert
Greetings, Co G	Strauss
Talent Show, T	Variations on a theme by Paganini
Schubert Waltzes, Co	Schubert
The Poet and the Muse, D G	Liszt
Awalking in the Woods, S	Irish jig
The Life of a Flower, S G	Lange
Not Wanted, S G	Walton
Prima Ballerina, S G	Strauss, Gounod
Portrait of My Mother, S G	music box
L'Artiste, D G	Casella
The Falling of the Leaves, S G	Byrd
It Starts with a Step, S	Handel
Strange Interlude, S G	Hovhannes
The Male and the Female, D G	Jezek
Bird, Wounded, S G	Varèse
The Come-on, D G	circus music, Zilcher, Bartok
Human Relations: Friendship, D G	Walton
Love, T G	Walton
Sympathy, T G	polka
Dance for Michael (Moschen), S	percussion
Useful Observations, Co	Badings, Raaijmakers, Ibert, Stravinsky
Too much Love, Co	Goslar
Bounces, Co	Irish jig
Child Prodigy, D G	Czibulka
Variations on an Old Theme, D	Byrd
To a Rose, T	Beethoven
Greatest of Ease, D	Boccherini
The Last Clowns, Co	Varèse
La Chasse (a Hunting Idyll), Co G	anonymous ballet music
Valse Very Triste, Co G	Sibelius

List of Works

Grande Tristesse, T G	Ellington
Splendor in the Grass, Q	Moondog
La Donna dello Dondolo (or The Swinging Beauty), Co G	Bayer
Collectors Items (a suite), Co	music box music
Lonely Bird, S	Mercier
A Dream, D	P. Henry
Pursuit of Happiness, Co	circus music
Circus Scene (Brecht), large Co	Mâche
All's Well that Ends...a suite, Co	sound collage, marches
All's Well..., Co	
Growing Up, S	
Nice Guy, S	
Survivor, S	
...that Ends, Co	
A High Lady, Co	Paganini
For Feet Only, Co	Irish jig
All the King's Men, T	Gluck
Auf Wiedersehn, Co G	Lange
Mercury, D	Havlick
Lovely..., T	hula music
Cupid II, Co G	McKenzie
Liebestraum, D G	Liszt
Pink Waltzes (suite), Co	Waldteufel
Never Too Old, S G	Cuckoo Waltz
Clown, Bruised, S G	Varèse
A Composer, S	bird sounds
A Daisy, S G	Debussy
Infatuation, D	tangos
Dancer (Like a Moth), S	percussion, medieval
HIM, Q	circus music
Ancestors, Co	Moondog
Mine Own, T	Lange
Strange Interlude, S G	Honegger
Ye Olde Story, D	music box

Children's Show Repertoire

Hello! Hello?, Co G	Strauss
The Flyinig Zucchinis, Co	Strauss
Don't Sneeze!, T	polka
Waltz of the Flower, T	Tchaikovsky

Happibirds, D	Zamfir, gypsy music
Square and Triangle, S	spoken comment
The Great Waltz, T	J. Morris
Hurry, Hurry!, Co	percussion
Magic, S	Walton
Happy Washday! S	yodeling music
Greatest of Ease, D	Boccherini
So Long!, Co	E. Strauss
Meany Milton, Co	Strauss
Happy Birthday, Co	potpourri
A propos Elves, D	Boccherini
Useful Exercises, S	P. Henry

Choreographies, etc., for other companies

Leggieros (Beethoven) – original ballet for the Hartford Ballet Co., also for companies in Milwaukee, Syracuse, Fort Worth and Tallahassee.

Charivari (McKenzie, Varèse, Colgrass) – a clowns ballet for the Joffrey Ballet Co., New York.

Die Fledermaus (Strauss) – choreography for the operetta at the Hollywood Bowl. Director: Val Rosing.

Babar the Elephant – choreography for the F. Waxman Orchestra at UCLA, Los Angeles.

Fiesta Pacifica: The California Story – choreography at the San Diego Balboa Stadium. Director: Val Rosing; Music: Meredith Wilson.

Galileo (Hanns Eisler) – stage movements and choreography for the American premiere of B. Brecht's play. Producer: E. T. Hambleton; Director: J. Losey; Starring: Charles Laughton.

Nightclub act for ballerina Joan McCracken.

River of No Return – incidental staging for Marilyn Monroe's film.

Pagan in the Parlor – world premiere of Franklin Lacey's comedy, co-starring with Moyna McGill and Doris Lloyd at the Pasadena Playhouse in Los Angeles.

Fairy Godmother – award-winning short film, designed and danced by Lotte Goslar; directed by Bobe Cannon for UPA, Hollywood.

Faust (Gounod) – choreography for the opera. Sarah Caldwell, conductor for the Opera Company of Boston.

Potluck and *Lallapaloosa* – two children's shows for the New York Shakespeare Festival. Producer: Joe Papp; Director: Bernard Gersten.

Clowns and Others Fools I and II – children's shows for the Batsheva Dance Company in Israel. Also for the London Contemporary Dance Company.

Camera Three (CBS) – half hour television program. Director: Merrill Brockway.
Dolly [Hass], *Lotte* [Goslar] *and Maria* [Piscator] – film documentary by Rosa von Praunheim.
Channel WGHB – half hour television program in Boston.
L'Histoire du Soldat (Stravinsky) – costume designs for the production at Tanglewood Music Festival.
Children's Ballet for the Accademia di Danza in Rome, Italy.
Vienna Lusthaus – co-starring in Martha Clarke's Music-Theater production in New York City (Public Theater) and Washington, D.C. (Kennedy Center).
King Lear, directed by E. Piscator at the New School in New York, choreography for the Mummers' Dance.

Ah, to live in the country! Sketch by Lotte Goslar

Lotte Goslar at home in Connecticut. Photo: Gary Gunderson

Self-portrait with pear. Sketch by Lotte Goslar

Index

A Man's a Man 98
Andersen, Hans-Christian 104
ANTA, Marathon Dance Festival
  (New York) 99
Armstrong, Louis 18
Artist in Person, The 33, 39, 95

Bach, Johann Sebastian 5
Baden Learning Play, The 98
Baker, Josephine 54
Balada z Hradů (Ballad of Rags) 33, 35, 36
Balanchine, George 151
Barnes, Clive xv
Bauhaus 17
Beethoven, Ludwig van 5
Beneš, Eduard 1
Berliner Ensemble, The 98, 148, 149
Berliner Staatstheater, the 148, 149
Bernstein, Arthur 25
Brecht, Bertolt xvi, 25, 97–105, 146–149
Breuer, Marcel 17
Breughel, Pieter 150
Brown, Forman 75, 77
Bruant, Aristide 121
Burnett, Harry 75

Cabaret Tingel-Tangel 25
Café Royale 101
Carlin, Kathleen xxi
Cannon, Bobe 81, 82
Carné, Marcel 82
Chagall, Marc 66
Chanin Theater, The 51, 52, 71
Chorus Girl 113
Circus Scene 97–104, 152
Cirque du Soleil 35
Clarke, Martha 115
Columbia Concert Corporation 51
Cole, Jack 54
Columbia University 52

Conversation with an Ant 111
Cukor, George 118

Debussy, Claude 72
de Mille, Rosalind 1, 150
de Mille, Agnes 54, 55, 150, 151
Dietrich, Marlene 43
DiMaggio, Joe 118
Disgruntled, The 21, 39, 51, 54
Disney, Walt 81
Dix, Otto 18
Draper, Paul 2, 54
Durov's Pig 97

Ellington, Duke 18
Enters, Agna 52, 53

Fairy Godmother 82
Fairy Tales 104
Fellini, Federico 7, 104
Felsenstein, Walter 148, 149
Fille de Joie 35, 36
First Dance 111
French, Gene xxi
From Vienna 54

Galileo Galilei xvi, 97, 148–150
Gambardella, Mary xxi
Gay, Galy 98
Gerald McBoing-Boing 81
Gert, Valeska 25
Giehse, Therese 29, 30, 43–47, 51, 148, 149
Gieseking, Walter 25
Ginger and Fred 107
Godino, Stephanie xxi
Good Soldier Schwejk, The 35
Goodman, Benny 113
Goslar, Erich 11
Goslar, Walter 8

Graham, Martha 13, 52–54, 151
Grimm, the Brothers 104
Gropius, Walter 17
Guardian Angel, The 35

Haak, Charles xxi
Havlik, Adolf 18
Hayes, Helen 43
Hee, T. 81
Hell on Wheels 55
Henning, Magnus 43–47
Hirsch Cabaret, The 29
Hitchcock, Alfred 86
Hogarth, William 150
Hollander, Friedrich 25
Hubley, John 81
Humphrey, Doris 54, 151
Hurok, Sol 52, 150, 151
Hustler, The 84

Institute of the Arts and Sciences 52
Intoxication 35

Jacob's Pillow Dance Festival 72, 98
Jaffee, Sam 54
Ježek, Jaroslav 35, 55
Johnson, Alvin 52, 54
Joyce Theater 21

Kabarett der Komiker 25
Kafka, Franz 98
Kandinsky, Wassily 17
Kaye, Danny 109
King Lear 54
Klee, Paul 17
Knopf, Alfred 47
Komische Oper, the 148, 149
Krauss, Ernst 52, 104
Kreutzberg, Harald 150
Koegler, Horst xv
Kokoschka, Oskar 37
KTLA (television station) 107

Lamour, Dorothy 85
Lanchester, Elsa 75, 77–79, 97, 148, 149
Landowska, Wanda 65
Laughton, Charles xvi, 30, 75–79, 97, 148, 149
Leigh, Colston 52, 54

Lenox Arts Center 115
Lenya, Lotte 25, 66, 99
Liberated Theater, The 1, 26, 33–37, 39, 41, 43, 55, 75, 95, 97
Little Heap of Misery 67–69
Loring, Eugene 72
Lyon, James 98, 102

McCarthy, Senator Joseph 81
McCoy, Clyde 67
Mâche, François-Bernard 101
McMillin Theater, The 52
Mann, Erika xv, 29–31, 41, 43, 47, 51, 54, 55, 97, 104
Mann, Klaus 30, 43, 47, 97
Maracci, Carmalita 72
Menschen am Sonntag (People on Sunday) 82
Mephisto 97
Mercier, Richard xxi
Miller, Arthur 1
Moholy-Nagy, Laszlo 17
Mondrian, Piet 14
Monroe, Marilyn 117–119
Morris Jr, William 54
Mozart, Wolfgang Amadeus 5
Mr Magoo 81
Mummer's Dance, A 54

Neuman, Dorothy 75
New School for Social Research, The 52, 54
Nightmare 67
Nijinsky, Vaslav 52
Noviny Spoutaneho Divadla (The New Chained Theater) 33

Osvobozeneho Divadla (The Liberated Theater) 33, 97
Ocko, Edna 54

Palucca, Gret xv, 13, 115
Pantomime Circus xvi, xxi, 21, 81, 98, 115
Peppermill Cabaret/Revue, The xv, 29–31, 33, 37, 41, 43, 51, 52, 66, 75, 97, 104
Pilobolus 115
Ping-Pong Cabaret, The 29
Piscator, Erwin 54

Potter, Dr Russell   52, 54
Prévert, Jacques   82

Quai des Brumes (*Port of Shadows*)   82, 84

Rainbow Room, the   54
Reich, Wilhelm   102
Reinhardt, Max   25, 43
Reunion in New York   54
Ringling Brothers, The   101
Robbins, Jerome   55, 151
Rockefeller Center, the   54
Rubinstein, Artur   65

Sahl, Hans   26, 43, 55, 66, 67, 82, 99, 120, 121
Sahl, Ute   120
Scarlatti, Domenico   5, 72
Schechter, Joel   97
Schiff, Paul   65
Schloss, Sybille   29
Schoop, Trudi   52, 53
Schubert, Franz   5
Seehaus, Bill   75–77, 79
Short Organon   102
Show of Shows, The   54
Sillman, Leonard   54
Seven Year Itch, The   117
Shakespeare, William   77
Shawn, Ted   72, 73
Shuftan, Eugen   82, 84, 85
Shuftan, Marliese   84
Siodmak, Robert   82, 86
Skala, The   25
Steinberg, Saul   123
Strasberg, Lee   118

Suddeutsche Konzertdirektion   65
Susanna and Jose   107

TAC (Theater Arts Committee)   54
TAC magazine   54
Tauber, Richard   45
Tiger Rag   113
Toulouse-Lautrec, Henri de   121
Tschaikovsky, Peter Ilytch   151
Tudor, Antony   151
Turnabout Theater, The   21, 65, 71, 72, 75–77, 81, 85, 97, 104, 117

Ullman, Tracy   78
UPA Group, the (United Productions of America)   81, 82

Verdi, Giuseppe   xv
Vienna/Lusthaus   115
Villon, François   35
Volksbühne   17, 18, 25
Voskovec, George (Jiri)   1, 26, 33–35, 39, 55, 95

Waltzmania   67
Weidman, Charles   54
Weill, Kurt   25, 99, 101
Werich, Jan   1, 26, 33–35, 39, 55, 95
West, Mae   117
Westergard, Lance   xxi
Who's Who   82
Wigman, Mary   13, 17
Wilder, Billy   82
Woodsprite, The   85

Yale Puppeteers, The   71
YMHA, The 92nd Street   54
Young Mother   35

Other titles in the Choreography and Dance Studies series

Volume 10
First We Take Manhattan
Four American Women and the New York School of Dance Criticism
Diana Theodores

Volume 11
You call me Louis not Mr Horst
Dorothy Madden

Volume 12
Dancing Female
Lives and Issues of Women in Contemporary Dance
Sharon E. Friedler and Susan B. Glazer

Volume 13
Modern Dance in France
An Adventure 1920–1970
Jacqueline Robinson. Translated by Catherine Dale

Volume 14
Anna Sokolow
The Rebellious Spirit
Larry Warren

Volume 15
What's So Funny?
Sketches from My Life
Lotte Goslar

This book is part of a series. The publisher will accept continuation orders which may be cancelled at any time and which provide for automatic billing and shipping of each title in the series upon publication. Please write for details.

For Product Safety Concerns and Information please contact our EU
representative GPSR@taylorandfrancis.com
Taylor & Francis Verlag GmbH, Kaufingerstraße 24, 80331 München, Germany

www.ingramcontent.com/pod-product-compliance
Lightning Source LLC
Chambersburg PA
CBHW080736300426
44114CB00019B/2606